Diary of a Red Devil

DIARY OF A RED DEVIL

By Glider to Arnhem with the
7th King's Own Scottish Borderers

Albert Blockwell

Edited by Maggie Clifton

Additional material by Niall Cherry & Robert Sigmond

Helion & Company Ltd

This book is dedicated to my father, the true author and to the memory of the heroes of the 1st British Airborne Division, who by their sacrifice initiated the Liberation of the Netherlands.

Helion & Company Limited
26 Willow Road
Solihull
West Midlands
B91 1UE
England
Tel. 0121 705 3393
Fax 0121 711 4075
Email: publishing@helion.co.uk
Website: www.helion.co.uk

Published by Helion & Company 2005

Designed and typeset by Helion & Company Ltd, Solihull, West Midlands
Cover designed by Bookcraft Limited, Stroud, Gloucestershire
Printed by Cromwell Press Ltd, Trowbridge, Wiltshire

This edition © Helion & Company Limited 2005

ISBN 1 874622 13 2

British Library Cataloguing-in-Publication Data.
A catalogue record for this book is available from the British Library.

For details of other military history titles published by Helion & Company Limited contact the above address, or visit our website: http://www.helion.co.uk.

We always welcome receiving book proposals from prospective authors.

Contents

Publisher's Note

The editor and publisher would like to take this opportunity to mention their thanks to two people who have greatly contributed in the preparation of this book.

Firstly a Dutchman, Robert N Sigmond author of two magnificent books on the 7th KOSB in the second World War, these books are 'Off at Last' and 'Nine Days at Arnhem' (the latter obtainable from Helion & Co). He graciously allowed 18 images from his books to be used in this work. He is also a volunteer helper at the Airborne Museum in Oosterbeek who also allowed for 8 photographs to be used from their extensive collection.

Secondly Niall Cherry author of 'Red Berets and Red Crosses' (also obtainable from Helion & Co), the history of the medical services in the 1st Airborne Division, who looked through the diary, wrote some explanatory notes and liaised with the Dutch connection. He is also the UK representative for the Society of Friends of the Airborne Museum Oosterbeek.

Between the two of them they have now assisted with over 20 airborne forces books.

Preface

This is a transcript of a diary kept by my father during his years as a soldier from February 1940 to his demob in 1946. He was a young, naïve 20 year old lad when he joined the army, but after participating at the Battle of Arnhem in Holland, being captured by the Germans and becoming a Prisoner of War, he eventually arrived back in England a mature, worldly man.

After moving up and down the U.K., experiencing life in the army as a raw recruit, the hard training and the comradeship of his fellow soldiers, like so many others he was eventually caught up in the realities of the REAL war. He joined the 1st British Airborne Division and was proud to belong to an elite force destined to fight in one of the most famous – and disastrous battles – in recent history.

In his own words, 'he was one of the lucky ones' by surviving the hardships that followed. He was transported in one of the many gliders, which descended on Holland on 18th September 1944, landed safely and immediately had his first taste of enemy combat. He fought bravely, but fearfully, as his comrades fell around him. He endured hunger, thirst and sleepless nights whilst they were bombarded with shells 24 hours a day. Inevitably, after 8 days, he was taken prisoner and realised the nightmare had only just begun.

He was then transported in a box-car and endured 6 days and nights of cramped, inhuman conditions to his first Prison Camp, where he spent, in his own words, 'the five most horrible weeks of my life!'

After enduring that introduction to Prisoner of War life, he was once more transported to another Camp in another box-car for 5 days and nights, in the same conditions as before.

Stalag IVB was to be his 'home' until almost the end of the war, when he managed to escape with a fellow Prisoner, and seek the eventual sanctuary of the American Army.

His exploits didn't finish there as he had many anecdotes to tell before his return to England. He was given 56 days leave, then received orders to report for duty again.

This book is not a fiction adventure, full of daring exploits, but an honest, fact-filled diary written from the heart. My father describes his feelings, observations and experiences, which could only be portrayed by a man who has 'been there, done that'.

My father went on to marry his sweetheart and lived a quiet, contented life with her for the next 55 years. In the past, a handful of close friends and family had been allowed the privilege of reading this book – without fail everyone who read this neat, hand-written diary was moved to tears by the content. After his death, my mother treasured it more than ever before. She would not let it out of her sight and I only acquired it on her deathbed. I would now like to share it with the rest of the world, not as a violation of his privacy, but out of respect for what he, and all the young soldiers in the Second World War, went through to make our country a better place for future generations.

Editor, Maggie Clifton, July 2004

1

February 1940

Chilwell, Notts.

On 15th February 1940 I had to report for Army service in the RAOC (Royal Army Ordance Corps) at Chilwell, Notts. I can't say I was sorry to go, for like most lads in those days I looked upon the Army and soldiers etc. as an adventure – just an experience. Of course, we didn't think of the war and battlefields. Most of us, like the people at home, thought it would all be finished in a few months. That was what newspapers and talk made us believe. They said Germany could not last more than 6 months – the people were starving, the country was bankrupt and anyway he was only bluffing, his tanks were only cardboard!

So we were all very light-hearted. Little did we know of all the things that were to happen in the coming years, of the setbacks, of the sacrifices many were to make, and the suffering there was to be in all Europe. Perhaps it was as well that we didn't – what would have been our feelings if we had known we were to do 6 or more years in the Army – not so much the time we had to do, but the conditions and hardships we had to suffer meanwhile? Learning our training the hard way, with insufficient and inadequate equipment and weapons and not even having a bed to lie on at nights. Had we started with full equipment and the proper training camps etc., our life at first would have been much easier, and perhaps the war would not have lasted the years that it did – but those are all 'ifs'.

Not that I, myself, had a very tough time – I had my hardships, and rough living along with the rest of the boys, but taking everything into consideration, I was pretty lucky. A lot of things happened, and at the time we often thought we were getting a raw deal, but strangely enough everything eventually turned out for the better – at least if not for the better, it could have been a damn sight worse. Of course, during the years some of the boys suffered more than I did and sorry to say a great many paid dearly, but as I said, myself – I always came out lucky.

Well, as I said, my Army life commenced at Chilwell Ordnance Depot. We arrived there that afternoon, and were met at the small station by an NCO who took us down the road to the Depot. We had a good meal right away and a radio was playing dance music in the dining hall all the time. At the time I remember saying, 'This is all a blind, just wait until tomorrow', but no, it was like that all the time. We were all passed through the various departments, filling in forms, medical exams, etc., and then kitted out with battle-dress etc. Then we were shown to our beds, which were in a big converted store building – so there were about 300 beds in that one part alone, but the place was centrally heated with wash places down the centre so we weren't too badly off.

We wondered how long it was going to take us to get dressed in that strange thing they had given us, the battle-dress, for when we looked at it, it seemed to be a maze of buttons and Oh! Those big boots! But the NCO's were helpful chaps or perhaps it was us that looked helpless. Anyway, the first morning they lined us up and had a look at us, gave us a hand here and there, taught us how to put on put-tees, etc. and were really decent chaps.

Well, we gradually got settled down to our new life and began to look on new fellows coming in as 'rookies', after all, we could now fall-in, and turn left and right all together, providing we all called out the time – One! Two! Three!

The first two or three weeks we had many laughs, many of the boys could not be completely dressed owing to awkward sizes, and so in the squad was somebody in civvy pants and Army tunic and next to him someone would have civvy jacket and Army pants. Then, of course, there was the inevitable chap who was thick in the head – the one who couldn't march, couldn't halt when everyone else does, and then when we used to laugh we'd all get it in the neck from the Sergeant.

Then the next trouble was sore feet and blisters – those new boots and that square bashing played havoc with our soft feet, so that 85% of us were hobbling like old men after the first week. At night we were content to just take off those boots and lay on the bed and sing to the accompaniment of a piano-accordion that someone had. The tunes that will always be associated with the boys of the Army training in 1940 – 'Roll out the barrel', 'The Quarter-masters store', 'I've got six-pence', 'The Siegfried Line' and many others.

Well, after 3 weeks we were supposed to be smart on the square, know the ins and outs of a Lee-Enfield rifle, and also know something about a Lewis machine gun (which was obsolete). So then we were posted away to different places on trade courses.

2

March–May 1940

Acton, London

I, along with about 70 others, went to Acton, London for a 12 week Fitter/Mechanical Vehicle Course. When we arrived there we were taken to a requisitioned church hall, which was our billet. Well, that wasn't so good. The place was like a dungeon, with a small washhouse for about 100 of us, but discipline was easy.

In the morning we made our way round to the workshop, where we had a roll call, and then breakfast, and then the classes began. We had civilian instructors and we had 10-14 days at each subject – engines, gearboxes, ignition etc., and as I was at my trade I rather enjoyed it. Also, after a week, I changed my billet to a big school, which was much more comfortable, and had good roommates.

By that time I had a service uniform and we spent good nights around Shepherd's Bush and Hammersmith. Most weekends we would get a pass to go into London and we often had a day in there. Of course, in those days the bombing had not started, but also there were not the canteens and service clubs that were to come years later. So it was not so enjoyable then, but round by the billets there were fish & chip shops and the usual 'Smokey Joes' eating place that seems to be in every town, so we didn't do too badly.

Lieutenant-Colonel L.F. Machin commanded the Battalion from 28 March 1940 until 17 July 1942 (Courtesy Robert Sigmond)

Towards the end of our course we had new Sergeant-Majors posted there and so discipline was tightened up a great deal, and then the fighting had started in France, so that things were changing all round.

During this time we had no equipment etc., only our change of clothes, and that civvy gas mask in the civvy container – we looked a queer crowd. Then rumours started about leave – on and off, on and off, – the Army was always full of rumours in those days. Well, in the end we did get leave and also our postings to units, and workshops, etc.

That morning I caught the tram along with my mates, down to the station and we were all looking at our individual orders, where we had to report to – I was to report to the 7th Battalion Kings Own Scottish Borderers[1]. Well, as I said to my mate, 'I'm due for a shaking up now, going to an infantry mob', but as I was to find out, it was going to be a lot easier than I expected.

1   The 7th (Galloway) Battalion The King's Own Scottish Borderers was a pre-war Territorial Army unit formed from elements of the 5th (Dumfries and Galloway) Battalion The King's Own Scottish Borderers in early 1939 when the TA was expanded. The first CO of the unit was Lieutenant Colonel The Earl of Galloway who was appointed on 17th June 1939. Mobilised on Sunday 27th August 1939 they were designated a 'home defence unit' and therefore did not go to France with the British Expeditionary Force after war had been declared. The unit remained in Scotland until early May 1940 when it moved to Marlborough in Wiltshire, where it only remained a few days before moving to Byfleet in Surrey. The 7th Battalion was part of the 44th Brigade 15th Division and it's CO since March 1940 had been Lieutenant Colonel L Machin.

3

25th May 1940

Byfleet, Surrey

While I was on leave I had notice to say the Battalion had moved to Byfleet, Surrey, and so had to report there. When I arrived at the station there was not a soul in sight, so I just started walking down the road towards the village. Well, that walk eventually lasted about 2 miles and me with a heavy kitbag too!

Then I had to cross two fields to where my Company, HQ Coy, were billeted in a requisitioned country mansion. I there met my two mates who had arrived before me, two more RAOC fitters, and we shared a small room with our three blankets on the floor for beds. There was no such thing as a dining hall, meals were dished out in the field into our mess tins, rain or fine, and we cleaned them the best we could with grass.

Our job was to maintain and repair the Battalion's transport – the same job that I was to have all through the war. The transport in those days was a few 15 cwt. trucks, a few motorcycles, 1 Bren carrier and a few civvy trucks – a motley collection if every there was, but we got them going, as inexperienced as I was in those days.

From that first day there I began to hear the bagpipes, morning, noon and night, but they were new to me then, so I didn't mind the terrible noises that came out of them!

It was very quiet out there at nights, only a small village down the road, a big change from Acton where we were out every night and having to run back to billet to get in before lights out. I ran down those streets so often at Acton, I knew just what speed I could safely turn the corner without sliding on the back of my neck.

But the weather was good those few days at Byfleet, and we were free-lance, no one bothered us and we had no duties to do, so we had good days driving around the country lanes, testing trucks and rather enjoying life.

While we were there, trains were passing through from the Channel ports bringing back men from Dunkirk – we looked at them but it didn't seem to stir us much. We didn't even realise the meaning of those trains, nor did we realise what those men had come through. To us, like the civilians at that time, the war seemed a long way off and we always had that feeling that somebody else would do the fighting and finish it. To us, life just went on from day to day, we never thought of demob. Sometimes we would wonder how long it would last, somebody would say 2 or 3 years and we would laugh at him and say, "What – 3 years in this Army!" Little did we know or even bother about in those days – we were only young, most of us 20 years old, just boys, but we were to come back men. Some were only boys when they went out there, but after a few days they were boys no more, they were men – men before their time, aged by hard experience and many seeing death on the battlefields. But such was our life to be, it had to come in our time, so there was nothing we could do about it – we made the best of it.

Well, after a week at Byfleet we were told we were to move, and moving in those days was some game, for we weren't trained in convoys, had insufficient maps, and very few knew where we were going. We just weren't trained as we were to know training in a few years time.

We eventually got moving along the road though, and our first stop was to be Tilbury Dock, where we were to use the ferry to cross over to Essex. When we arrived there about 5 trucks were missing, lost on the road, so we had a wait there for a few hours until they caught us up.

4

June 1940

Coggeshall and Witham

We managed to form up on the other side and off again, making for a little place called Coggeshall. All the time we were passing the womenfolk, they would throw us kisses and blessings, thinking we were from Dunkirk. They had a right to, when they saw the conglomeration of junk we were riding along the road.

We reached our village and were split up into threes and fours and billeted in a civvy house. The lady was very good to us and we had a room to ourselves with beds and sheets etc. – it was a good billet. Our transport was all in a field on the outskirts. At that time we had no spares, no MT Stores, in fact, still not organised at all.

We only stayed there three days and then moved on again to a place about 12-15 miles away, Witham, a small market town. Our billets there were in a big hall. We had three blankets on the floor as usual and were pretty crowded. We there mixed in with the rest of the MT boys for the first time. Most of them were Scottish, from Dumfries district, and at first they seemed pretty rough, but as we got to know them we settled down with them better.

The first night we were there the air-raid siren sounded. We were a bit excited at first, but just laid where we were and nothing happened. I got to know two or three boys from Newcastle district there – Tom Pearson, Tom Bell and a few others, and of course my other two mates Jim Fuller and Ken Smith were with me.

Well, we no sooner got to know our way around there when we were told we were to move again. In the meantime a small Italian lad was sent away from us, which made us think something was happening in Italy. That month Italy entered the war with Germany.

5

June–August 1940

Abberton, Essex

After a few days there we again moved to a place near the Thames Estuary, Mersey. The Rifle Companies of the Battalion took up positions near the beach, while the transport and us were about 2 miles back on the main Colchester Road at Abberton crossroads. The transport was again in a field and we were billeted in an old church. We were crowded and washing was done in a bucket of cold water outside the door.

We still could only do minor repairs as we had no stores – I did not even have rifle or equipment up to then. The Rifle Companies were far from fully equipped – they only had rifles and a few Bren machine guns, certainly not enough to face an invasion which was then imminent. But Hitler missed his chance, he did not try to land. It was strange because even in those days we never thought of being defeated. At the back of our minds we always seemed to have that confidence that he would never come and we would win.

We now looked forward to two or three more years to do before the war would finish and when someone would mention 1944 or 1945 in the papers we would still laugh and make fun of it, not thinking it possible.

There was a little pub where we were and most nights we would congregate in there and have a good singsong. Just after reaching Abberton we were made up to strength by 400 boys from the Yorkshire & Lancashire Regiment, and a big majority were Londoners. Amongst them was Tiny Birch, a six-footer who was good with a ukulele he had with him, and he was the life of the party. We made good pals there – Danny, Fred Barrel, Fred Yoe and others and Breckenridge who was broad Scottish and used to go up and down the scale when he talked. Then there was the showman Hughie Leak, he could beat anybody on the dartboard – he was killed in Libya the following year.

Colchester was about 5 miles down the road and so that was our usual place of entertainment at the weekend and sometimes through the week. We were not allowed so far away without a pass but we started taking a chance and dodging off and I continued taking chances from then on in my Army life. In those days the restrictions were not on transport as they were later and we would spend many an afternoon riding round the lanes on motorcycles in our shirtsleeves and no one to bother us.

Bombers then started coming over at night and most nights we would stand outside and watch the searchlights and Ack-Ack lighting up the sky towards London. A stray bomb or two was dropped nearby, but as we had never experienced bombing or the danger of bombs, we were not scared.

Well, the weeks passed on and we just lived like that from day to day, and having a little fun at night, and then after 10 weeks we moved again.

6

August–October 1940

Colchester, Essex

This time we moved into a real camp about 1 mile outside Colchester, Roman Way Camp. It was a good, hutted camp, with a canteen, gym, workshop and a big square, much to the regret of the Company lads, but that didn't affect us. The huts were arranged in squares, with baths, lavatories etc. all in the centre. We had good nights in those huts – regular 'fights' would take place at night, somebody would throw a bed biscuit at someone else and that would start it. The room would divide into two and then the biscuits would fly – then the next hut would come along complete with pillows and we would have a good set-to for a few hours – that's how it went on regularly nearly every night. I had lost a good mate there, as Tom Bell had a bad smash on a motorbike and was badly smashed up in hospital.

When we went out at night there we had to sign in and out and carry gas masks and tin helmets, but we soon wangled that and slid out past the guardroom. Then coming back late we would either chance getting past the guardroom via the back

Tom Bell, Albert (centre) and Tom Pearson, Colchester, August 1940
(Editor's collection)

19

of the trucks or else go past the camp and then cross the field and crawl through the hedge, which was all done in pitch dark.

Whilst in Colchester at night we had to walk around with gas masks on our chests and tin hats on if the sirens sounded, which was every night, so you can guess what we said about that! We soon got to know of a quiet way back to camp, up past Le Cateau Barracks and round the back of some other camps and across waste-ground and moorland and so dodge red-caps, so that was our favourite way back. We were nearly always passing these barracks when the bugles were sounding Last Post, so we had an idea of the time from them.

We had many narrow squeaks from being caught, but always managed to get in, usually to find that the bed collapsed as soon as it was touched, or else the blan-kets would be tied in the centre or something like that. It was quite normal to find the bed full of junk when I came in late, rifle, boots, brush, old bucket, scrubbing brush and anything else handy were usual things to be found in bed. Then I would probably not find a thistle until I got right in. Yes! We had our fun those days – fun that one couldn't possibly get at home in 'Civvy St.'

Then the Battalion started it's training, the start of training that was to last for over 4 years. At first the Battalion would go out for the day on an exercise – the boys often marching all day. It was often very funny because the CO and everyone would go out and then a dispatch would come in and the DR would not know where they were and had to ride all round the district to find the CO.

We spent many a day in the summer riding out on motorbikes. There was a training area nearby and we would have a good time riding around there covered in dust and dirt, but enjoying ourselves. That was the best of us Fitters, we were free to go out anytime with trucks or motorbikes, nobody paid any attention to us, and if we were stopped, well – we were 'testing'.

While we were there the daylight air raids started and often we had a grand-stand view of the whole show. I remember one day we heard a terrible drone in the sky and we went out to see and we could just see those little black dots in the sky, but there were hundreds of them – stretched out over the sky as far as we could see. As we watched we felt no fear from them, because we did not know the danger of bombing, and there was always that thought that it was somewhere else that was going to be bombed. Then the Hurricanes and Spitfires could be seen going up to meet those bombers – pitiful few that they were – but for all they were outnum-bered they made a toll of the Jerries. We would often see a crippled bomber drop-ping down, down till it crashed nearby, or see one pass overhead all ablaze with a 'Spit' on it's tail. It was then our turn to dash out on anything handy and bring in the crew if possible, or to salvage such things as engines and guns and bring back to camp.

Those weren't bad days at Colchester – we also had a fairly good stores with us then too, and a good MTO, Lt. Fairbairn. The Sergeant was the only 'fly in the ointment' – Sergeant Robb, he was a cocky, clever, little fellow who had a dislike for all Englishmen. He was Scottish, and especially disliked us RAOC fitters, as he didn't have much say over us and I guess that riled him. Anyway, we didn't pay much attention to him and just kept ourselves out of trouble, but at the same time being as awkward as possible to get our own back.

Well, the weeks passed by and then we were told we were going back to the coast for a spell. In the meantime we had 10 or 12 new 15 cwt. trucks added to our strength, but we were still far short of our full strength, as was the whole Army. For the RASC transport consisted of old requisitioned buses, and I remember when the men used to climb in with all their equipment. The old buses often refused to move, so half would have to get out and push to get it going – but equipment was coming through slowly.

7

October–November 1940

Clacton-on-Sea, Essex

The next move was to St. Osyth, about 1 mile from Clacton-on-Sea. The Rifle Company were billeted all round the district, some in Butlins Holiday Camp, some in bungalows. We were in a row of bungalows and the transport stood in the unmade road outside, feet deep in slimy mud. Our workshop was a tarpaulin nailed to the rear of the house, but we still couldn't do major repairs. Not that the vehicles needed it, as they were mostly brand new. We were kept busy making modifications – a small light had to be fitted to the rear axle of all vehicles for convoy work, so we were kept busy fitting these on. Then the motorbikes were under constant repair, so they were a full time job. We then got a new Transport Officer, a Captain Chance. He was a slave driver. He would have us working every minute of the day, didn't give us time for a cup of tea, and that wasn't all – he was the most sarcastic Officer I ever had the misfortune to meet. Like a lot of others, he had too much favouritism, and I wasn't one of his favourites.

We got quite a bit of bombing there at night, although only 1 bomb dropped close to our billets, and that set off a glorious fire just down the road. I remember us all down there watching the fire when another plane was heard diving down. There was a pillbox at the side of the road and when we heard the whistle of the bomb we all tried to get into the door together, so that about 5 were trying to get into a door 2 foot wide at the same time. By the time we got untangled the bomb had dropped with a thud nearby and had not gone off.

We were cosy in the billet there, we would have a roaring fire on at night and Jim Fuller had a radio of his own there, so we were O.K. as far as comfort went. The only trouble was, every time a bomb dropped within a mile of us at night it shook the bungalow and burst the cistern pipe in the loft. So it was a regular job every morning to solder the water pipe upstairs.

I had a weekend pass with Tom Pearson one weekend and Fred Yoe's people had a pub in Bethnal Green, so we arranged to go through on Ken Smith's motorbike. It wasn't so much the trip to London as the experience of seeing the London blitz at night that made us go. We got there O.K. and spent a good day with his people, and then about 6 pm we noticed everyone making their way down the street to the subway. We weren't long in following. The folk went down the subway and Fred's brother, Tom, and I dropped in the pub across the road. We weren't in long before the barrage started, the lights shook, the windows rattled, the glasses shook and then I started shaking. Tom and I were both of the same mind. We thought it was time to get underground, well underground. So we drank up and made across to the underground station. We went down the first flight of stairs and stayed a while with the wardens talking until a big one dropped too close to be healthy. So we went down farther still to the platforms and there I saw the people laid in one solid mass. Men, women and kids and blankets from one end to the other. Boards were laid over the lines and steel watertight doors were closed at both ends and the air was stifling. The glazed walls were dripping with moisture and at the end of the platform were the lavatory buckets, screened off, and they didn't help the atmosphere.

After seeing that I was thankful I wasn't a civvy living in London and I also thanked God that my people at home were spared that. Those conditions alone must have been the death of many of those people, especially the young ones.

After riding back through the rubble and glass out of London we eventually got back to camp, having a skid outside Colchester first and landing in a heap, but we were not hurt.

8

November 1940–February 1941

Haverhill, W. Suffolk

So after 6 weeks at St. Osyth we were to move again, inland to a small town south of Cambridge, called Haverhill.

Here we were once more crowded into a hall behind the church – the rest of the drivers billeted above a pub. The Companies were again round the district one or two miles away. The transport was lined around the playing field and the office and workshop was in a requisitioned yard and sheds, which wasn't too bad as we had a bit of cover.

The town itself was only small and had a canteen and two very small picture houses, but there were plenty of pubs, which suited most of the lads. Of course, I spent many a night in them, but usually only for somewhere to go and the company.

We were not there long when a good few of the MT boys were drafted away to other units for overseas service. At this time we were in the 15th Scottish Division of which our Brigade, the 44th was part together with the 6th KOSB and the 8th Royal Scots. The other two Brigades were the 45th and 46th Brigades. Also attached were the usual support units, Engineers, Artillery, Medical and Signal units and so on. From now on we really started training as a Division.

We had a few weeks to settle in and most of us had leave, having to take all our equipment with us FMO (Field March Order) and kitbags, so we had quite a time getting home in those days. Once in the train the fun would start. First we would get jammed in the corridor and then the gas cape would come undone and after making progress for a few yards would suddenly be brought to a halt. Someone would be stood on the gas cape tape. Then someone's rifle would go through a window, and so on. It was quite a journey in those days.

Then, as I said, the training started. We would go out for 3 or 4 days at first on exercises. Mostly it was training for the Officers in tactics etc., for we would be out all the time and not know what was happening or where we were going. Us fitters often travelled in some of the MT trucks, sometimes we would have a truck of our own for breakdowns, and often we were kept busy, for it was winter by then and the country was pretty bad. Sometimes we would stand around in farmyards all day long, freezing cold, nothing to eat, and nothing to do. Then after dark we would have to move, groping about in pitch dark, trying to see the truck in front and probably finish up in the next farm a few miles away. Then we would try and get a bit of sleep. If we were lucky we would find a hay-barn and climb on top of that, or inside a cart with a bit of straw. Wherever it was, we couldn't take off equipment or boots, which were usually wet through. Then the ration truck would turn up and that meant finding mess tins and eating in pitch dark and the stew was often bad or stone cold, so we would be 'browned off' after that.

When I look back now and think of the way we lived then and what we put up with, it amazes me how on earth we ever stuck it. We spent night after night like that, week after week, month after month, and we just seemed to take everything as it came. We moaned and groused and laughed too, but we just carried on. It seems strange now when I think, but in those days we were not long in the Army and not very old. So of course as the years wore on we learnt more, got a little older and were more easily sick of the whole thing.

9

Christmas 1940

Well, the time was close on for Christmas now, and we were talking about being home for the following one. I got friendly with a young lady in the GPO there and at Christmas her people were good enough to invite Danny Ransley and I to tea and a party. They were good people and we certainly appreciated their kindness.

We weren't given much respite before we were out again on more 'exercises'. We sure took some punishment that winter – 3 or 4 days every week we would be out, sleeping where we could, usually too cold to sleep at all and thankful when the dawn came. Often we would spend the night digging trucks out of snowdrifts, frozen stiff and feet wringing wet. Yes! We had our hardships in those days without going more than 20 miles from the billet.

10

New Year 1941

Then New Year came along – we had a good night in the pub that night and really made merry, but the following day I had to go to the Carrier Platoon at a little village about 4 miles out of town, Stoke-by-Clare was the name.

Well, I was pretty 'browned off' leaving the boys – the Carrier boys were mostly strangers to me. I hated the sight of those Bren Carriers[1] – they were awkward to work on, cold and clumsy things, I detested them, but as usual I just had to make the best of it.

I was billeted there in an old house, sleeping on the floor as usual, and nowhere to go at nights. Many a night I would get changed and walk down the road about 2 miles to a pub just to pass the night away. I would have a pint and then walk back (I was not a big drinker). Yes! I spent horribly, miserable nights there, when I think now of having to live like that it makes me shudder. I would go crazy if I thought I had to spend days and nights as I did then.

I used to look forward to the days on exercises there, for they helped to pass away the weeks quicker. Although at the same time I dreaded the thought of spending nights in those Carriers. It was not so bad while we were moving, for we would stretch a ground-sheet over the top of our heads and get plenty of heat from the engine and just doze away the time. But when we stood at the roadside for hours it was murder. We would spend hour after hour stamping up and down trying to keep warm and probably getting soaking wet while we were doing it. No! That was a wicked, miserable time I had then and it was much the same for a long time to come.

On exercises too things were getting worse, for we were not allowed to sleep in barns and haystacks – although we usually did crawl in on the quiet. The only trouble was, if there was a move through the night we would not be wakened and the first thing we knew was the noise of the trucks starting up. Then we would have a mad scramble, scooping up blankets and straw in the dark and climbing into our

1   The original role envisaged for the Bren Gun Carrier (or to give its official title the Universal Carrier) was for a fast, lightly armed vehicle to carry infantry across ground denied by small-arms fire. As well as a driver and observer it could carry a number of passengers and in particular the Bren gun teams found in all infantry units. The vehicle became universally known as a Bren Gun carrier. Made of approx half inch plate it was powered by a V8 water cooled petrol engine which developed 85 bhp. It was about 12 foot long, 6 ft 6 in wide and 5 ft 2 in high. It weighed somewhere around 4 tons. The engine size was over 7000 cc and had a fuel tank of 20 gallons. When travelling on roads the fuel consumption was around 7 miles per gallon. It had the advantage of being of relatively simple construction so it was able to be made by most of the UK major automotive manufacturers. It was also made in large numbers in Australia, Canada, New Zealand and the USA. It is reputed that more carriers were made than any other British 'armoured fighting vehicle'. After having suitable modifications two carriers could be carried in the huge Hamilcar glider.

trucks as quickly as we could, and probably get a bawling out from the Sergeant Major if he saw us come out of a barn.

I could well understand the farmers complaining about damage to crops etc., for this sort of thing was going on all over the country. No sooner would one unit move out of a farm, and we would move in the following night. Usually the first thing the boys would do would be to make a recce around the hen houses for eggs. They would even milk a cow if they could get hold of one. Then in the barns, hay and straw was strewn all over and then some fool would start smoking and start a fire. So there was little wonder the authorities had to clamp down on us.

After a few weeks at Stoke-by-Clare the Platoon then moved down into Haverhill again. We had huts round a field on the edge of town, so it was better for us at night. But the huts were very cold with concrete floors and high double bunks. The wash-place was about 5 minutes walk away, together with the dining hall. Often we would get washed in a small stream at the back of the huts, but after a while this dried up.

Before I moved to the Carriers we had a run of accidents in the MT. First Jim Fuller had a smash going home on a motorbike, but he was O.K., and then Ken Smith had a smash at home one weekend. He lived at Cambridge. Then shortly after that I smashed a Guy 15 cwt. truck.

I was coming back to town one wet day when a dog ran into the road in front of me, just opposite to where some lads were lined up for tea. Well, I put on the brakes, but the old truck just slid along like a skate. I could see I wasn't going to miss the dog. Well, that wasn't bad, but just then one of the boys ran into the road for the dog, so there was only one thing to do and I did it. I swung round straight into a corner of a house. The truck swung round and flung me out and wrapped round a lamp-post. When I got up I got a terrible shock for there was a heap of boys on the road and in those few seconds I imagined I had killed some of them. I imagined being charged with manslaughter and prison and everything, all in those 2 seconds. I had caught one lad with the tail-end and he had got knocked into all the others, knocking them down.

Well, for that I was on a charge – first I was in front of the MTO, the next day I was in front of the Company Commander, and a few days later in front of the CO.[2] It wasn't the fact of being in front of the CO as all the inspecting and routine we had to go through first. Police escort, march here, march there, hat off, repeat this, repeat that. I was a bundle of nerves before I went before him. But I was lucky enough to get off with that … only to have another smash the following week.

This time I was taking Fred Barrel up to Battalion HQ with 8 gals. of petrol in the sidecar. Well, everything was O.K. for a mile or so and then I came to a left hand bend and that's where the bike decided to go straight on – and straight on it went, clean through a hedge and full tilt into a ditch. I didn't know a thing from leaving the road because I was knocked out and they told me afterwards I was pinned underneath the bike.

All I knew was when I came round about 1 hour later I was soaked in petrol and I realised how lucky I had been that the bike did not catch fire. Well, I had to go all through the same routine again, Orderly Room, CO's charge etc., but once again I was let off.

2   The CO of the 7th Battalion at this stage was Lt Colonel L. F. Machin.

While at Haverhill we started our inoculations and vaccinations etc. Once more I had been lucky again, for most boys are inoculated and vaccinated as soon as joining up, but we never were. So it was my first and I took it pretty badly. Somehow I was missed for vaccination.

At this time too we had started doing PT (physical training) in the mornings. That was one good thing about our Battalion, an order would come out and it would be strongly enforced for a week or two and then everyone would forget about it. The first few mornings we had PT we turned out in the dark. The Company Commander and MTO and all the Officers were out. The Sergeant Majors, Sergeants, everybody – full strength. That was for the first 2 or 3 mornings and then the Majors would get fed up, and then the Junior Officers. Then after a week or two the Sergeant Majors would stay in bed and so we would be left with one Sergeant to get us out, and by the time he got us all together in the dark, which was quite an achievement, it would be breakfast time. Then after a while it would drop off completely. Until one morning the RSM would come round and find us all in bed and then it would go on for another week.

Baths were a queer do there. We had the use of a Woollen Mill for a bathhouse – in one part there were 3 or 4 big tubs, and we would get undressed alongside the civilians who were working, and we would get into these tubs, four in at a time. It was quite a job washing your own leg and not someone else's!

A motorbike Platoon was attached to the Carriers there, and about the last week in Haverhill a mate of mine was made Fitter I/C of them. Bill Kerr was his name. He came from a farm at Coldstream on the Scottish Border. We chummed on together quite a lot. He was a good lad, blonde and always laughing. He laughed at anything, sometimes at the wrong time. For often on parade if the Sergeant Major was screaming orders out, I could often hear Bill Kerr chuckling under his breath and then it took me all my time to keep a straight face. We used to call him 'Laughing Boy', but he was a good chap to have along with us, he often cheered me along at times.

Then, about the end of March the rumours were that we were going back to the coast. We were thankful for a move for we knew it would keep us off exercises for a while. We thought exercises were pretty rough, but really we had an easy time compared to the boys in the Rifle Companies, the infantry boys. We had the cold and rough living to put up with, but remember, all the time we were stood around waiting, these infantry lads were doing the marching and taking up positions, etc. Then at night we were always lucky enough to have a truck to sleep in, or at the worst, underneath it. Also, while we were riding mile after mile these boys were foot-slogging. Often we would pass them on the road and they would be out in the rain, laden with equipment and weapons, trudge, trudging, mile after mile.

I often felt sorry for them, so even though we had our bad times, those chaps were always a damn sight worse off. I never forgot that – I always thought how fortunate I was that I didn't have to do that marching as they had to. Even when we were in camp and just working ordinarily, those infantry boys would often be out on day exercises, so heaven knows, they must have been 'browned off' an awful lot. Even when not out training they would be drilling, hour after hour, when we were taking things easy and thinking what an easy time we were having. So as bad as it was at times, there was always a hell of a lot of lads having a worse time, even here in Blighty.

11

March–November 1941

Lowestoft, Suffolk

About the end of March we moved to Lowestoft, Suffolk. Here the Rifle Companies had positions all along the coast and we were a bit luckier, as our garage and workshop was in the centre of the town and the billets were only 200-300 yards up the main road. The Carriers were dispersed around the local playing field or rather ex-cricket field, but I did most repairs in the MT workshop.

The first few days we were there all the Carriers were in a lockup yard, but a few bombs soon made them think again and disperse them and it seemed like the cricket field had to suffer. The MT had a good garage, for they were in a requisitioned body builders place. So that all the transport were able to park in and around the yard quite easily. Also there was a good workshop, roomy and light and complete with benches and a forge and all the tools that had been left by the civilian firm.

Albert (centre) 1941
(Editor's collection)

Albert (centre, front row) 1941
(Editor's collection)

For the first few weeks I was with the Carrier Platoon, and so I was billeted with them, along with Bill Kerr. Our billets were in requisitioned houses all along the main road and usually 3 or 4 men to a room. But we had no beds, so the floor was still as hard as ever, but by that time I had worn my hip square so that it didn't feel so uncomfortable!

What's the news? Albert (right) 1941
(Editor's collection)

Relaxing. Albert (left) 1941
(Editor's collection)

There was plenty of entertainment in the town. Four or five picture houses, two or three dances, four canteens and plenty of pubs, so there was something for everybody. So every night we were out as soon as possible and usually our first stop would be the canteen on the front, where it was possible to get egg and chips and chocolate (at that time they were not rationed). Then we would go to a Picture House or else have a night with the boys in a pub.

Having a laugh. Albert (left) 1941
(Editor's collection)

Giving support. Albert (in supporting role) 1941
(Editor's collection)

12

Day and Night Air-Raids

During the day we had Jerry over regular – every morning about the same time we would hear a drone coming in from the sea, and we would stand in the yard and watch for him. He would often circle right round the town while every gun in the district had a shot at him. But I don't think anyone ever hit a Jerry – not those first two or three months. Of course, before he departed he would drop a stick of bombs somewhere. Lucky for us they always dropped in another part of the town, because we never took cover, we were too fascinated watching him.

For the first few weeks we were never bombed at night, although he passed over regular, going inland, and then one night we were coming home from the pictures when we heard a Jerry diving down. We stood and listened for a few seconds and then we heard the swishing whistle of bombs coming down. Bill and I dropped to the pavement, but lucky for us they were incendiaries. Hundreds of them burst over the roads and houses. First they gave a loud 'pop' and then burnt with a brilliant flame.

We hurried along to the billet, and saw everything was O.K. there, so we went up the road to give a hand with the houses on fire. Some civvies were managing a bungalow alright, so Bill and I ran up the road a few yards to where an elderly man was calling for a hand from a bedroom window. We rushed upstairs to the room that was burning and found the old man doing his best with all the junk that was on fire. It was only a small room, and it was full of everything it shouldn't have been – papers, boxes, bedding, everything inflammable. So the first thing the other lad did was to knock out the window and we threw out everything that was on fire. The bomb was lodged in the rafters, so it was hard to get at, but the other lad thought he could put it out with a bucket of water. So we passed him one. The mistake we made was standing in the room watching him, for as we might have expected, he missed the hole and the water hit the ceiling and made a good job of soaking us. So we passed him another bucket. This time I stood outside the door, just in case. But he managed better, then in the darkness we passed him another bucket, but it was full of sand. So we all stood watching expectantly for the deluge of water when the bucket of sand flew in every direction.

That started Bill off laughing – which eased the tension a bit, because I was listening to another Jerry droning over the town and was feeling rather inclined to get downstairs under cover a bit. But hearing him laugh made me forget the danger for a minute. We finally left the old man to keep an eye on it and then had a walk around the streets for a while as we didn't feel like going into the house while anything was dropping. So we stayed in the street until it was over. It was only a short raid so we finally got to bed and spent the rest of the night peacefully.

The following morning at work we told our stories to each other and had a good laugh, as we often did – the morning after.

I then started to work on the MT again, as they were pretty busy, so I moved my billet down to the MT boys. I got a good billet, I shared the room with three Tyneside lads, Joe Welsh, Vince Lilley and Tom Seaton. They were good mates.

35

Upstairs there were more Tynesiders, in fact there was only one Scottish lad with us, Peter MacFarlane. We often threatened to throw him out, saying he was a foreigner.

Tom Seaton in my room was a queer old stick – not old, actually, but looked old and had old ways and stubborn and cantankerous. If we wanted the door open, he would want it shut and vice-versa, we had many a 'barney' in there with Old Tom. They were all good lads though – honest and straight – all of them.

The Council had thoughtfully removed the gas meter in the cellar but we soon made a 'modification' down there, by knocking big nails into the wall to carry a bracket. Then fixed an extension to the main gas-pipe, so that by turning on the main pipe, we just lit the end and boiled water for shaving.

Over the road was the 'roughhouse' billet. All the roughest, mischievous lads seemed to get into that one billet. There was 'Tich' Millar, Snipe Edgar, Teddy Woodcock and the pip of them all, McSherry. McSherry didn't give a damn for no-one or nothing. He had a peculiar habit of not being able to wake up in the mornings. Whether he was faking or not, I never did find out, but anyway he was so good he used to get away with it. Some mornings the Sergeant would try to waken him and he just wouldn't, no matter what they did to him. Then the Sergeant Major would have a go and then the MT Officer himself would go up and see him, but no! Old McSherry still snored peacefully on – sometimes until about 10 am. He was a lad if ever there was one. If ever there was any trouble at all, the first thing the MTO did was to call McSherry and a few of his mates in the office and ask them where they were and what they were doing at that time. Had he not been such a damn good worker, when he did work, he would have got thrown out of the MT inside a week.

Well, so much for the boys, they were a good crowd, taking all round.

The transport was now a full-time job, modifications were being made every week, for at this time the fighting was on in the Desert and new methods were being tried out at convoy work both in training and actual warfare. Usually by the time we learnt a new method it would be amended by another order. So that went on for years, while the Armies were training at home, first one method, then another.

We were kept busy painting all the transport. They had to be painted a certain way and then the design would be altered again, while a different type of camouflage was tried. Then plates had to be fitted to all trucks for convoy work. The Division sign would be on one side and 'PASS' on the other. It was a stupid idea that was never used, and was just another example of waste in manpower and material that went on in the Army.

Then there was a great period of 'bull' – all trucks had to be like show-pieces, engines had to be polished up, pipes brasso'ed and so forth. We often used to shake our heads and think 'Here we are, up to our neck in War, total War, and should be training every minute' but instead we spend months polishing trucks and doing nothing. It just seemed as if the 'High-ups' were just content to start doing something maybe next year or the year after.

As I said before, this only applied to us in MT, for all this time the Company boys were on guard day and night along the coast, stand-to every morning and night, so they were probably thinking different to us.

13

June–August 1941

We often had 100% stand-to's in the early morning and dusk, which meant we all turned out. We stood by transport all ready to move, and strangely enough it was often on these stand-to's that we were caught by Jerry. Then we would load a few trucks with sandbags and they would have to drive up and down the road looking for incendiaries.

It was on such a night that the Carrier lines were straddled with Anti-Personnel bombs and three of the boys were hit, but not too badly. We were always lucky, for not once were the transport lines, or any of our billets, hit.

I used to be terribly scared during a raid at night. It was the waiting and nervous tension that got me. I would often lay in the billet on the floor and listen to the drone of his motor, waiting and listening for the whistle of bombs. Hardly daring to make a noise breathing, waiting! Waiting! Listening, my heart pumping like a hammer and then he would go. Then a few minutes later another one would come over and all that tension would start again. That was what broke a fellow's nerve. Although I was scared I always stuck it out, and during a raid when he started diving down, I would listen to him coming, waiting and probably hearing the whistle of the bombs. My legs would literally shake, my knees would really knock and I couldn't stop them.

I remember one lad 'Toosh' McLaughlan, used to take his blankets into a civvy shelter every night and sleep there. The Sergeant Major threatened him many times about it, but 'Toosh' was more scared of the bombs than of the Sergeant Major!

After one particularly bad night, when a few big shops were burnt down, including Woolworths, I went on leave the following day, and never was I more thankful to get away from a place than I was there. I dreaded the thought of coming back but I had to. Dad was commencing his holidays the day I came back, so he came back with me, as he was going to Norwich. Then the following day he came through to Lowestoft and then at the weekend I had a 'pass' through to Norwich, so it made a break for me.

The summer months and hot weather was then coming on, so we spent most of our weekends in the sea, bathing and laying on the sands. We often went down at night too. We would have a few cakes at a small shop just across the road from the workshop and then into the sea. On Sunday mornings we were often down there about 10 am and we would stay there for the rest of the day, having a few snacks at the canteen nearby. We had some fun on the beach those days. We would often lay and watch the antics of McSherry & Co. with a boat that they would endeavour to launch. The Crazy Gang weren't in it! We really had some good fun and laughs on the beach in those days.

Another pest at night were the mosquitoes. The room at night would be full of those things. We often used to close the door and window and then all have a 'blitz' on them and so get rid of most of them – only to have the sirens go again and face another night. We often laughed though, because we now had double bunks and I was on top of Seaton. When Jerry came diving down I would often be out of bed and on the floor in one leap – often on top of Old Tom, who would be out seconds before me. But we didn't stop to curse when we heard the whistle of those bombs – we just hugged the floor and waited. We didn't sleep very much those nights, for after the sirens had sounded I just couldn't go to sleep. I would lay listening and straining ears and nerves for every noise.

We had some people living next door to us and they were always afraid, as there was no man in the house. There was the mother, two daughters and Granny, so every night when the 'banshee' went, the young girl (she was 17) would come to the window shouting for Joe. Joe Welsh used to go in and sit with them in the shelter in the garden. After weeks of that poor old Joe would pretend he was sleeping, and we would all lay quiet in bed and she would be calling 'Joe, Joe' at the open window. Still no move from anyone. 'Joe, Joe', then Old Tom would reach the end of his patience and he would suddenly give such a shout 'Get the hell out of it, Joe!' For we each knew we were all awake, and Joe would then reluctantly climb out of bed, cursing in his way. Joe only said 'blow this and that' or 'rot it', or sometimes a strong 'sod it' – never anything stronger.

They were good people to us though, for during the dark nights they made tea for us all in the billet and one of the girls would come in with the tea and cups all on a tray. She would just walk right in with it and if there was no one downstairs, she just came straight upstairs. No warning, so she often surprised one of the lads changing his pants. She would often hear some strong billet language too, but I think she was too innocent to understand it. In fact, I'm sure she was.

Bob Henderson, one of the drivers, was on the ration truck so that we always had plenty to eat at night. Every day he would drop in with the nights rations – bread, butter and anything that was on the menu that day, and of course kept the people next door supplied with tea for us, so we fed pretty well in those days.

There were some other people over the road who we got friendly with too. Well, it was the girl I got friendly with, only neighbourly friendship though, for I never went out with her. They were very strong Church people.

I remember one Sunday she asked three of us across for tea. It was a lovely tea and they were all very homely, but after the tea we knew what to expect. They started to get ready for Church.

Well, we were determined that we wouldn't go walking down the road with all the family, not past all the other billets. I could picture what those billets would have been like had we gone. Each window would have been full of faces and remarks – no, Sir! I couldn't face that, not even if I wanted to go to Church. So Joe Steele made an excuse that he wanted his hat and gas mask and was out the door before anyone could stop him. Well, Tom and I tried the same technique but there was nothing doing. Mary wouldn't let us both go and she was a bit offended I guess, when she knew we didn't want to go to Church. So we didn't feel too pleased about walking out on them after the tea, but we didn't feel pleased about going to Church. So we eventually got out of the door and didn't stop until we got to our back garden, ready to disappear in case she came over the billet for us.

Well, that is just one of the many little experiences we had in the Army. There was always some little things like that happening, but that one time seemed to stick more than the others.

At this time we had another Fitter join us, Bill Eaves. He seemed to be very quiet at first, but he was O.K. after a while and didn't care for anything. He just took everything as it came, one of those lads that seems to live from day to day, and never worrying about what tomorrow would bring.

We had a lot of convoy training then. Night convoys were very frequent. We would all go out in convoy and tour around the lanes for a few hours, often getting lost, and cursing everybody concerned.

The day convoys were the worst, for in daylight every time we stopped we had to draw in to the side and camouflage, and that meant throwing the big netting over the truck and then cover sides with grass, weeds, etc. This had to be done on all exercises. We would no sooner get the nets over, than the order would come to move. Taking those things off was a different proposition to putting them on, for they would catch on every bolt and sharp corner, and maybe would be caught up in the branches of a tree. So it meant climbing up on top each time. This was alright if we had to do it two or three times, but then we had to keep on doing it two or three times every hour until we were thoroughly 'browned off' with nets, trucks, exercises, everything.

14

October–November 1941

Well, the months passed by at Lowestoft, the summer came and passed, autumn came on, still no sign of a move. We were not wanting to move. It was a good town, we had good billets, a lot of the boys were well in with the people and a lot even married there, so we were content there.

Then, about the end of November after being there for 9 months we started to plan for a big move. Rumours were coming round every day. All moves and destinations were now Secret, so we were left guessing as to where it was going to be. It was to be a big move, we knew that much, taking perhaps 3 days, and all the Division was moving, which meant a lot of planning, and for us a lot of convoy training and rehearsals, mostly at night.

Eventually, we moved off one morning about 5.30 am. The men were mostly in troop carriers, RASC trucks, the Carriers went by rail. We had a parting bomb from Jerry the night before we went, and that hit a big pub outside the station. Also during the last week there we had three heavy bombs drop on some bungalows just up the road from us and they did not explode. So it was the job of my cousin, Ernie's, Bomb Disposal Company to lift them, so I was lucky enough to see him for a day.

So all that we knew of our new station was that it was about 260 miles away, and the first stop was Grantham.

We made fairly good progress during the day – averaging about 12-15 m.p.h. Convoys cannot travel faster than that, for in a big convoy the rear trucks are having to average 30-35 m.p.h. to make up for trucks slowing up or stopping all down the line, and that line was a good length. Each Battalion had a strength of roughly 130 vehicles and there were three full Battalions in each Brigade and other units on top of that, RASC, RAOC, RA, RE's etc. Had we moved in one convoy, the whole Division, the first truck would be in Northumberland when the last truck was leaving Lowestoft – such was the motorised transport of an Infantry Division. So we split into three convoys, on three different routes. Thanks to the Movement Control CMP's the route was unmistakable. We had a certain colour to follow and at every corner of that journey there was a flag and arrow pointing the way. Then, as we approached Grantham the first night MP's were at the road ends with lights, so that it was well organised, and no-one was lost at all, which was quite a change with our Battalion.

That night we drew into an Estate about 2 miles outside of town. As usual, there was about one foot of slimy mud and of course it was pitch dark and no lights allowed, so we just sloshed around in this slime the best we could. The first job was to fill up with petrol, which meant stumbling up to the head of the column and then struggling back again with two 4 gallon tins of petrol each. Many of the lads would get fed up of carrying the two heavy tins and dump one over the hedge. Petrol was thrown away in gallons in that place.

I was pretty lucky as I was travelling in comfort in an old requisitioned Austin 16 h.p. saloon car, so that night we had the comparative luxury of the car seats.

We managed a few hours sleep and then at dawn we were on the road again. This time we travelled up the Great North Road, making good time all the way. We had one or two trucks breakdown but were able to get them going and catch up with the convoy farther along the road.

The second night we made Catterick Camp and pulled into an empty camp there. We parked the trucks and then made our way to some damp, dirty, empty huts, where we had to sleep on the cold concrete floor, if we weren't too cold to sleep.

The next day we were on the road again and hoping to get through before dark. We by-passed Darlington and Bishop Auckland and on up to Rothbury and up the main road again towards our destination, which we were now pretty sure was somewhere around Wooler, but we were still not certain.

15

November 1941–July 1942

Wooler, Northumberland

Well, Wooler was our stop. At least it was the nearest habitation to our camp, for we stayed in a place called Ewart Park, about 4 miles outside.

The camp looked pretty grim when we got there. There was a big square field surrounded by a thin wood, and amongst these trees were the huts. The washing facilities were a couple of open troughs and cold water taps, which weren't exactly anybody's idea of comfort as it was now the end of November and very cold up there in the hills. There were even no lights or blackouts on the huts for those first few weeks, so we were all pretty miserable.

The first thing we had to do was to find some sort of a workshop, and we had the use of a yard at the end of the Battalion HQ building, which had once been the house or Manor of the estate. We managed to fix up a tarpaulin in one corner of the yard and had a couple of benches, so we just had to make the best of it and be prepared for a rough winter.

Jim Fuller was there made up to Sergeant. The MTO, Capt. Chance, had put him through for it, for he was one of Chance's favourites, or as we would call them, 'crawlers'. Chance would not even put me through for a 2nd Class Trade Test, not that I cared very much. I didn't want any favours from that man and I didn't want to feel humbled to him in any way, anymore than the necessary respect to an Officer.

We had a few changes in NCO's etc. now. We had an old Indian Sergeant in charge of us now, in place of Robb and I wasn't sorry to see him go. The new chap, I forget his name, was pretty cushy. He was inclined to be a bit 'windy' of Officers etc., as those men often were. He was a regular and had his job and rank to think about, not like us duration of War lads who didn't give a hoot for anything or anybody. We were only in for as long as we were needed and then back to 'Civvy St.', so tapes didn't interest the majority of us lads, especially if they were going to hinder us from having a bit of fun.

In the MT Store we still had Sergeant Ronnie. He was another regular and a two-faced crawler. Oh, yes! We certainly had a bright selection of NCO's in the Battalion then. Ronnie was in charge of Stores though and had nothing to do with us. He also had Jimmy Reid in there with him and a few other lads from time to time. The Stores were very much like the rest of the administration parts of the Battalion, or even the Army. They would be all organised O.K., shelves divided off, labelled etc., so that Jimmy could put his hand on any part that was needed. Then Ronnie would have some new ideas or someone else would and the place would then be upside down for a month before they were sorted out again. That was how it went on as long as I remember – always changing this or that.

We now had a Lieut. Wallace as 2nd I/C of MT now. We had another one at Lowestoft, a Lieut. Melville, but wasn't much good in any way. Wallace was young and at first seemed to be pretty harmless. I will say this for Chance – he had the transport well organised and nobody had a say in the matter beyond the CO and 2nd I/C. But with Wallace, as I say, he was young and a bit scared so that the Sergeant Majors and a few more had more power over us later on when he was MTO.

We were beginning to get settled in and we had changed our billet for one down near the Battalion HQ, which didn't please us very much. But we were near to a wash place down there and the dining room. Also we had electric light, which the other huts didn't have, so we were better off in a way.

There was nothing to do at night there, only go out to Wooler, a 4 mile walk and we did that pretty regularly. We would get ready at night and set off walking down the road just as if we were going round the corner to the Odeon or somewhere, instead of a 4 mile walk. Then only to a half dead little place with half a dozen pubs, a small canteen and a small Cinema show. But we used to do it three and four times a week and thought nothing of it. We often went there at night just to have a couple of drinks and then walk back. It was not for the walk or the drink that we did it, it was just for something to do at night.

Sometimes we would have a walk up the other road about 2 miles to a little pub at Millfield, anywhere to pass the night away, for it was certainly dull and miserable in those huts at night.

We then started the inevitable 'exercises' for the winter months. It seemed to me like we only did these exercises during the winter months, for we very rarely did any during the summer. It appeared they were just endeavouring to put us through all the hardship possible, to make crocks of us in later years!

Well, I didn't mind the exercises there, because they passed away the nights and weeks. Anyway, we often had more fun on the exercises than if we stayed in camp. We put in some cruel days and nights up in those hills around Wooler. We often went out for three or four days. As usual the MT would be crawling along, start, stop, start, stop, all day long. We would be sat in the cabs frozen stiff, feet aching with cold, unable to sleep at nights, but we were now better organised for food etc. The rations and cooks travelled along with each convoy. I think during those months I slept in every different place possible. I slept in truck cabs, in the back of trucks, in the hedgeback, under haystacks, in barns, in rain, snow and sunshine. I often said to my mates, "If we don't suffer after all this, we certainly should do" for we did practically everything against good health possible. We laid and slept at nights in wet pants, wet boots, sat shivering all day long, laying on the damp ground. I was sometimes lucky on these exercises, for on the small ones, we didn't all have to go out, so we took it in turns to go out one at a time, so that when everyone else was away the few left in camp would have an easy time.

We now had another Fitter join us, Jim Brooksbank, a Yorkshire chap, and he was put on the Carriers.

It was quite a journey to go on leave from there, as we had to go by truck to the main line, which was 12 miles away at Belford, unless we were lucky enough to catch a bus to Newcastle. After a while we soon got organised in matters like that. Being in the MT it was nearly always possible to get a lift anywhere. One of the lads, usually McSherry, would take out a truck at night, unofficially, to either Belford or Berwick, so we always managed to wangle anything at all. It was the same in the mornings – round about 10 am each day there would be a small convoy of trucks go down to Wooler to a small café 'Harry Fox's Rendezvous Café', where he sold smashing egg or bacon rolls, 4d. each, and a good drop of tea. So at that time each day it was impossible to find anyone in the lines at all. Then the M.P's had to start clamping down. Then, of course, after someone had been on a charge, a watch was kept on the lines by our Reg. Police. So it fell back on us Fitters a lot then, for we were free to go in and out of camp anytime with trucks on the pretence of 'testing' or going for spares. So when we went out we would have a full load in the back.

16

Christmas 1941

It was now drawing close to Christmas once more, and we wondered what we would get for it, anything extra, what holiday?

We didn't get much in that place. We had a bit of a tea down at the Carrier Lines, where there was a big hall available. That night I believe a few of us went into Wooler and had a few drinks – nothing out of the ordinary.

Snow was becoming pretty deep and we had a little old building that had once been a cottage for a workshop, so that all trucks were outside, deep in snow. I remember turning out many a morning and the trucks under repair would be feet deep in snow. It just about broke my heart to look at them. Even at night we hardly had enough coke for the fire to keep warm, and the huts were draughty and damp. Yes! It was pretty miserable living in those days. I don't know how we ever had the spirit to stick it.

The boys were now having a good time at nights, for most nights of the week a few sly trucks would nip out of the top of the woods and away up the road to Coldstream on the Scottish Border. There they would have a few drinks and then away to a dance in one of the villages. All the lads needed was petrol, and amongst three or four of them they could wangle a few gallons each day, on the work tickets. Then at night take off the speedo cable, so that no mileage was recorded.

They were caught a few times, once when I was with them, and we were all in front of the MTO, but as most of the lads were his 'crawlers' we were let off. It wasn't too bad at first because only one or two trucks would go. Then later it got to five or six trucks every night, and then two of the lads had a bad smash when they were drunk. They were Court-martialled and got 28 days 'over the wall', so that quietened most of them down a bit. One of the chaps who was in the smash was 'Geordie' Johnstone. He could get away with murder. When he was driving he hardly wore a hat and always had his tunic neck open and wore a bright coloured scarf round his neck. He was told about it many times, but more often there was nothing said to him and he would get by anyone dressed like that. He was the same all the time I knew him. I don't remember seeing him dressed properly once – when he had everything else on, he would have 'civvy' shoes on his feet! He would defy anybody, and he got away with it.

17

February 1942

Derby

About February I got notice that I had to go to Derby for a Fitter MV Refresher Course for three weeks. I was pleased to get away from there, if only for a few weeks. I had to take all my kit with me, including blankets, which was quite a load, and I knew all about it when I had it all on my back.

However, I got there eventually and befriended two lads who I knew by sight. We were billeted in a big house and the classes were held in a school along the road a little way. The course was very interesting and instructive for me. The only trouble was the parades we had to do three or four times a day.

We made up for that at nights, for every night we were out in the town and spent most nights at the roller skating rink. It was a good town for entertainment, good Picture Houses, and for us – plenty of girls – so I was sorry when the course

On leave at Stockton. Taken on 6th May, 1942. Five years later to the day he became a father of editor Maggie (Editor's collection)

was finally finished. However, I had learnt a good bit on the course and it had been a good break to get away from the Battalion for a few weeks.

I returned to the Battalion to go straight onto a big exercise – was I cheesed! I travelled with Bill Kerr in a 30 cwt. truck, and I think I spent most of the time grousing about exercises and everything connected with them.

So it went on, for weeks and months, exercises, nights in Wooler, miserable nights in those Nissen huts, and then the summer was approaching. PT was started again, every morning at Reveille we were out on the field – I hated turning out for PT but once I was out in the early morning sunshine and fresh air, I enjoyed it.

We spent a few Sundays down at a stream nearby where we were able to have a little swim. I was not a good swimmer, but could keep myself up.

There was one thing about these exercises, we saw plenty of new countryside and new places we had never before seen. Usually the bigger the exercise the better and easier time we had, for in a Brigade or Division exercise our Battalion would perhaps be out of action for a day or so while another part of the Division tried some new tactics. So we were able to lay around in the sun, or maybe have a night out in a nearby village! We had many good times out on exercises as well as bad, even at the worst of times there was always something to laugh at.

The rumours of another move were now starting to circulate. Every day it would be somewhere different, Newcastle, Morpeth, all round the district. It was amazing how rumours and news did get around in the Army. I suppose pubs and canteens were where most of it was picked up, lads from one unit would know something and we'd know something else and put two and two together and there it was.

18

August–September 1942

Alnwick, Northumberland

When we moved into Alnwick, our next station, I don't know whether the Battalion slipped up again or whether it was planned as a take over in action – our Battalion made an exercise out of anything. Anyway, the poor old Company lads had to footslog and we had to follow up with the transport, so what a day that was! Alnwick was about 18 miles from Wooler, which was far enough with infantry equipment on. Of course, I sat it out in a truck and was punished by having to 'net on' every time we stopped. We only moved about 2 miles at a time, stopping every half hour, so we called those nets plenty that day!

When we reached Alnwick we drew into an Estate on the edge of town. The trucks dispersed amongst the trees and there we had the inevitable old hot-pot stew and then left to ourselves to find a 'kip'. We were unable to sleep in the back of the trucks as they were loaded, so most of the lads slept three or four together under groundsheets or under trucks. Three of us laid together under the tailboard of our truck, one lad laying on top of the tailboard. Of course, we made the necessary precautions to the bed before we turned in, spreading gas capes over the top in case the rain came on again – and it didn't disappoint us. About 2.00 am I woke up to hear the lad up top scrambling down cursing and then I moved myself and found the reason why. I must have made a nice little channel when I moved and so a nice little pool of rain calmly trickled down and circled round my feet. However I didn't know of a better hole to go to, so there I laid and soaked.

When dawn came it was funny to see the lads crawling out from soaking blankets and seeing someone standing up holding his pants behind away from him – yes! We certainly got a soaking that night. We weren't bothered about being wet, all that worried me was getting the blankets dry again so that I could lay in them that night.

We finally moved into the town that morning and we were shown the workshop and billet. The dining hall was in the local town's Drill Hall and Dance Hall and our workshop was underneath that, a big double door leading out to a road behind. All the Fitters were shown a small flat above a corner shop, there were two small rooms on the first floor, one containing a sink and the other just big enough to take two single beds, although at first we slept on the floor. Above us were two more rooms, Bill Kerr and Bob Currie in one room and the MO's driver, Bill Woods, in the other. Across the road from us a house was taken over for the MT office, but was later used as the MT store, which suited us better as we then had no Officers snooping about. The workshop was dry and plenty of room. What was more important – we were away from everybody, so that we were not bothered by anybody during the day.

We started in the morning about 9.00 am and most days we didn't see an Officer or anybody, just an occasional driver maybe, and then at meal times we only had to go upstairs and there it was. Jim Fuller had his radio in the billet too, so it was quite homely.

In the mornings we had no Reveille, usually the first thing we knew was hearing the feet of the Mortar and Pioneer Platoon lads marching down the road to breakfast and then we had to move fast.

At night we had no-one to check us in, we just rolled in whenever we pleased, although we were supposed to be off the streets by 10.30 pm. We didn't bother about that much, for after we had been there a week or so we knew our way around the town. So that if we were out late, perhaps taking a girl home, we could cross right over the town without touching a main street, keeping to side streets and alleys that were numerous in that old town.

We hardly ever stayed in the billet at night as there were two good Picture Houses and two good canteens and plenty of good pubs where we could pass the night on the dartboard with the lads. Then, after coming out of the pub or Pictures we could have a good fish and chip supper in the town or tea and cakes in the corner Café, which was soon known as 'Smokey Joes'.

Around 10.30 – 11.00 pm every night that place would be crowded out and outside would stand two or three policemen, waiting for their regular nightly job of going in throwing out someone who was arguing or fighting. It was funny to watch them – someone would start a heated argument in the back room and start jostling about. Then 'Smokey' would blow a whistle that he had handy and in would come the cops. All we could see would be their helmets pushing through the crowd and then out they would come again with two khaki Balmoral hats in between them. They would then propel them down the steps into the street – that was the regular routine every night after the pubs turned out.

A pleasant Sunday could be had by the walks around the gardens of a local Estate or along the river bank, which was usually crowded on a Sunday afternoon. Alnwick was the most picturesque and pleasant little town I've been in up North.

We had the usual exercises, but not so long and regular as we had been having them. They were mostly only one day Battalion exercises and did not affect us at all. Sunday mornings would often see a 'battle' in the streets with the local Home Guard, but we usually watched from the window.

I managed to get in another leave from here, which was a bit handier for me, as buses ran regularly between Newcastle and Alnwick. There was a good train service from there too, so after the usual argument when we were due leave, I managed to get mine O.K.

When I got back, there were rumours of another move. This time we were getting a bit shaky for numbers were stencilled on kitbags, so we knew we were in for a boat journey, but we were pretty sure it was only somewhere around Blighty. Most of us had the 'needle' again too, but it was only the usual Blighty inoculations, so that sort of verified the rumours that it was not a move out East or somewhere like that.

So after spending about six weeks in Alnwick we were finally given orders to pack up and be ready to move. We had to have our kitbags handed in one Sunday night and the following morning we were told we were to hand in blankets and then confined to billets. Orders came round that we had to parade at a hall at 1.0

p.m. in Full Marching Order (FMO). This we did and then we were all taken round the Picture House and were given a free show.

From there we went back to the hall, where we had a 'slap-up' tea, and then we were given our haversack rations. We got a boiled egg, a couple of apples, meat pie, cakes, sandwiches and a bar of chocolate. We sure thought our birthday had come, for usually a haversack 'gag' consisted of a couple of dry cheese or jam sandwiches.

We were then told to parade at 6.30 pm, so away we went for a final couple of drinks in the old pub until about 6.15 pm. Of course we were late in getting back – everybody was lining up on parade when we dashed up! We threw equipment on and got into line and the sights there were! Somebody had a pair of boots dangling from his pack, somebody else a coathanger, somebody with a bayonet sticking across the pack. Oh, what a collection! Then they had a roll call and as could be expected, McSherry & Co. were missing.

We stood there swaying for about ¾ hour and then, with the Pipe Band in front, we marched off down to the station. A surprise met us at the station for there were hundreds of people there waving us Goodbye. I didn't think the boys had made so many friends in so short a stay, but there they were. In the meantime, McSherry & Co. had come chasing along in the rear with the Sergeant Major behind them – they didn't care for no one.

We lined up along the platform in groups of six and then blow me if the train didn't pull into the opposite side! Trust our Battalion to do something like that.

Well, we finally got aboard and settled down for a long journey. We travelled all that night and finally reached Invergordon, way up on the Scottish East coast, the following noon.

We were then marched up to a transit camp and had a dinner there, then in the afternoon we were marched back to the Quay where the one-time Channel steamer 'Amsterdam' was tied up. We boarded her and were we crowded. I was with 15 others in what had been a small saloon on the top deck. I didn't mind so much, because I would rather be up on top as down in the bowels somewhere. Well, we didn't get far, because as soon as we started to move in the dark – crash! Sirens blew, alarms sounded – we had hit another ship, so after lining up at lifeboat stations for an hour we finally docked again and marched back to camp.

We stayed there for a week, doing parades, PT and route marches, until we were 'browned off'. What a desolate, wind-swept place Invergordon was. It often amazed me as I travelled and saw these places, why people lived in such places as this, but I suppose like everywhere else, it was home to them, and home is home, wherever it is.

Well, we finally boarded again, this time the sister ship, the 'Prague', and this time we made the trip O.K., apart from the usual Pentland crossing and seasickness.

19

October 1942–June 1943

Sumburgh, Shetland Isles

The following afternoon we sighted our destination, the Shetland Islands[1]. We were up on deck watching the Destroyer escort and 'Spits' flying overhead, when we began to sail up the coast of the mainland.

We docked at the one town, port and capital, Lerwick, where transport was waiting to take us to our camps, which were at the South of the mainland, Sumburgh Head. I had by then seen some wild, bleak, desolate country on my travels, but nothing like the bleakness of those Islands. They were just rocks, mountains and peat bogs standing in the sea between the Atlantic and North Sea, and we knew all about it too!

The Battalion was split up into small camps, a Company near to each Radio Station in that area. The area around the huts was a sea of mud and the Nissen huts had no lights and were leaking and draughty. There was no laundry facilities, so that all our clothes had to be boiled in old buckets on the stoves in the billet and then hung across the hut where it dripped all over the beds.

Being surrounded by the sea as we were, it was so damp it seemed to soak into our very bones. Blankets, clothes, everything was damp – if a box of matches was left on the shelf for a morning they were useless in a few hours. We bought candles at a small house-shop nearby and at night we each had a candle balanced on the bed-head, and tried to read or write by that.

Our workshop was a Nissen hut with one end taken off, so it was plenty cold. We often had to work with all our issue on, that was gum-boots, two pairs of socks, heavy underwear, pullovers – and oilskins on top of everything and still the cold and damp seemed to get through.

There was always a high wind blowing up there and when it was cold, that wind just seemed to go right through clothes and everything. The same in the billet, the wind whistled in one end and out the other. Then regularly every week a gale would blow up and then we knew what a wind was – it often blew at 90 mph. Huts blew away, trucks would blow over and it was nearly impossible to walk against it, the wind would pin me against a hut just as solid as if a truck was backed against me. When walking against those winds it was quite possible to touch the ground in front as your body would be bent forward so much. I always remember a crack one of the lads once said about that place. He said 'Well, what do you expect?

1   The Army troops posted to the most northerly islands in the United Kingdom, the Orkneys and Shetlands, were known as The Orkney and Shetland Defences (OSDEF). Their place in the 44th Brigade in October 1942 was taken by the 11th Battalion Argyll and Sutherland Highlanders. Once on Shetland the Battalion was spread out over a number of locations. Perhaps the most important place on the island was the RAF airfield near the village of Virkie, near which Battalion HQ was located. A Company was at Scousburgh, B at Ward Hill, C at Boddam and D at Quendale.

That wind comes 3,000 miles from America with nothing to stop it until it hits us!' – and that just about explains everything up there – surrounded by 3,000 miles of Ocean and open to all it's elements and moods.

Our only interest up there was waiting and watching for the mail-plane every morning and then every Wednesday fortnight waiting and watching for the leave-boat coming over the horizon. Our huts were on high land overlooking a big bay to the West and between us and the high Southern Peak of the mainland there was a strip of low, flat land, practically on sea-level. On that strip was the airfield, which consisted of two runways and a couple of hangers. The strength of this 'drome was only about six Spitfires, but it was also used by the civilian Scottish & Allied Airways Companies, and it was these 'planes that flew the mail in every day. Those men could fly – often when the Island was blanketed in fog, those 'planes would come over and fly round and round looking for a break, and then finally fly off again, much to our disappointment – 'no mail today!'

A new Corps was then formed, the REME[2], and so our badges were changed, and about the same time – lo and behold! – I got a stripe, which meant a rise in pay for me. The REME workshop in the Shetlands was in Lerwick, so we often had a run in there for spares etc. and were able to have a look around the small shopping centre and down the docks where there was often a submarine tied up. I once had the opportunity of seeing the biggest submarine in the world, the 'Severn', and we were shown a few compartments of it, which was quite interesting.

The natives of those Islands were a bit hostile towards us at first, they didn't speak or have anything to do with us, but after a while we got on speaking terms with them and then found they were very good to us. Dotted over different parts of the Island were clusters of stone cottages, primitive and filthy places. Each one would have a small plot of land around it, with a few vegetables and maybe a cow or goat tied up and a small hen run. That was how those old people existed, just scratching a bare living out of a bit of land, nowhere to go to, nothing new to see. For fuel they dug peat from the peat bogs that covered the Island. It was a common sight to see an old woman, wrinkled with age, dressed in old, black things down to her feet, bent double, and toiling on the land or carrying a heavy sack of peat to the cottage.

We used to go round to these cottages and buy eggs, so after a while we got to know some of these old people very well and I think they looked forward to seeing us and having a chat with us for a change. It was a bit difficult at first, because these

2   The official birthday of the Royal Electrical and Mechanical Engineers (REME) is 1st October 1942. Before this date the maintenance of Army equipment had been the responsibility of several different Corps. For example whilst the RAOC which in 1926 had been given responsibility for the repair of AFV and some other mechanical transport. But the Royal Engineers, Royal Signals and Royal Army Service Corps were still allowed to retain their organisations for repairing most of their vehicles and specialist technical equipment. In 1941, a Cabinet Committee was set up to investigate the use of manpower in the three services. As a result of one of its recommendations- that the repair services in the Army should be rationalised- the Corps of Royal Electrical and Mechanical Engineers came into being on 1st October 1942. By the end of the war in Europe in May 1945 the Corps had approximately 8,000 Officers and 152,000 Other Ranks.

old people spoke in a sort of Gaelic and some with a touch of Norwegian, but we managed to understand each other eventually. It was a regular job each day to go out with a truck and call round to these cottages for eggs. It was quite common to come back with six or seven dozen, which would then be divided amongst the boys in the billet, so that every night we would have an old frying pan on the stove and have egg and toast for supper. The bread and butter we could often buy at a small house-shop nearby, or else bring some back from the dining hall after tea, so we fed pretty well up there and most of us put on weight. I, myself, weighed close on 13 stone while I was there. There was a good canteen close by the 'drome, a Church of Scotland canteen, where we could get a supper at night, and often we went down there to sit and listen to the piano for a few hours at night. There was also a cinema on the 'drome where we could see an occasional picture or RAF show. Also, we had a mobile cinema show in the canteen once a week, so that we didn't do too badly, in spite of the roughness of the place. We often had a torpedo squadron come in to the 'drome at night and then in the morning we would watch them take off and fly out for Norway.

During those winter months we had the rare experience of seeing the Northern Lights in all its splendour. Then, during the summer months, we had constant daylight – about midnight the sun would rise again and start another day. 'The Isles of Nightless Summer' was the name given to those Islands.

I often stood and looked out to sea in the early mornings, and the sight was really beautiful. Over in the East the sun would be glistening over the North Sea and then to the West the horizon would still be in complete darkness. They were truly wonderful sights up there, but at the time we didn't really appreciate what we saw.

We were kept very busy on the transport up there. During the summer we worked until 8.00 pm every day and Saturday afternoons, and had Sunday off. I was content to work at night because the time passed more quickly and gave me something to do at night. At that time we were having a lot of trouble with the Carrier Platoon, for Bill Eaves had been up there for a while and he had got fed up being with them and come back with us.

However, Major Hill (the Mad Major) had ideas of his own, he wanted Fitters to go up there each morning and supervise the maintenance. We had got rid of Capt. Chance there, he volunteered for REME, and now Major Hill had to come and make himself a nuisance! He was as 'batchy' as anyone could be and still be loose, he was not even allowed a gun! When the boys were on parade he would turn to us and, with a suspicion of a tear in his eye, would say, sort of apologetic, something about him not allowed to carry a rifle. It was quite a common sight to see men of the Anti-Tank Platoon manhandling heavy anti-tank guns along the road, because he was short of petrol for the trucks, and anyway, he said, it was good exercise for the men! He would often come down to our lines needing a shave and minus one gaiter – yes! He certainly was nuts, but I give him credit, he was a soldier. When the boys were marching or going over an assault course, he was there in front with a pack on his back. He never told the boys to do anything he couldn't do himself. He was too mad to know when he had had enough and was dead beat, I guess – for often he would be marching out in front and the poor boys would be stumbling along behind, dead-beat but not daring to fall out.

I had two leaves from the Shetland – and what a journey! We were taken to Lerwick on the Wednesday and boarded the boat, crowded as usual, often laying on the deck of a saloon, which was sometimes better than having to suffer the heat of below decks. After being seasick most of the night, we would dock at Invergordon the following morning. From there we would march up to the transit camp and stay there the day and then get a troop train at night to Edinburgh, finally landing home the following morning, Friday.

It was the same going back, we had to catch that boat two weeks later on a Wednesday, for that was the only one that went up there, otherwise we would be absent 14 days and be charged as such.

The second time I went by 'plane from Sumburgh to Dundee and so was home the following morning, it was worth it to miss that boat journey.

While I was on leave, the Battalion moved, we knew we were moving but it was impossible to find out where to. Of course we all hoped the mainland somewhere, but the usual rumours were that it was to the Faroes or someplace like that. There was also a faint rumour of the Orkneys, but I think it was only by luck that somebody picked on that place, for that was to be our destination. So whilst on leave I was notified to report to Thurso, the most northern port of Scotland and from there to Kirkwall, Orkney.

20

July–October, 1943

Kirkwall, Orkney Isles

So, after 9 months in the worst place in 'Blighty' we moved one step nearer the mainland again, the Orkney Islands.

Our camp was about one mile from the small town and port of Kirkwall. This wasn't a bad little place, there were two Picture Houses and two good Canteens in the town and three or four smaller WVS Canteens and, of course, four or five pubs. These were a blessing to most of the boys, for there was no pub in the Shetlands, I guess prohibition was still on there.

The camp was very good, concrete paths and a square for parades, a canteen and a hall in the camp for dances or picture shows, which we had every week. The Rifle Companies A.B.C.D. were again in other camps two or three miles away, so we were on our own with HQ Company and BHQ, so things were always a bit easier when we were away from the other Companies.

There was a big REME Workshop a mile or two up the road, so we were handy for spares. Also, we were now well organised with the maintenance. Each Rifle Company had an NCO driver in charge of repairs and maintenance, so that all we did was make a weekly visit to each Company and see that everything was O.K. and if necessary detail a truck to come into our Workshop for major repair.

The country itself was much more pleasant too. It was just like 'Blighty', fields and trees, of which there were none in Shetland. There were also two or three small villages on the main road where we were, between Kirkwall and Stromness.

The weather too, was much milder – it was still pretty windy and rough at times, but that could be expected as we were still in the middle of the sea. From the camp we could stand and look out across Scapa Flow, the number one base of the Navy, so we often had wonderful views of the Destroyers of the Fleet coming in or going out of the bay.

Also on Sundays we were allowed to go over to the anchorage in a ferry and were allowed to board one of the ships and have a look around, which was quite interesting. The very sight of those big capital ships and all the scores of Destroyers and Submarines and smaller boats laying there, with the balloons and anti-submarine booms all round was just fascinating to say the least.

The Orkneys was a good station taking all in, for the advantages outweighed the disadvantages. We had the free issue of 50 cigarettes and matches and chocolate per week and the usual censored envelope. Also leave of 14 days was regular every 12 weeks, so that we were better off in those respects than many places on the mainland.

The leave travel was well organised too. We boarded the boat at Stromness and had a 2-3 hour run over the Pentland Firth, where we docked at Thurso. Transport then took us to the transit camp where we had a good tea and was able to buy chocolate at the NAAFI. Then at 6.00 pm we were taken to the Station where troop trains were waiting, so that we were home the morning after we left Orkney and had 14 days. There were many men worse off than that on the mainland.

I applied for a First Class Trade test at the REME Workshop there and had it and passed O.K., so I couldn't get any better without leaving the Battalion.

Those Islands were very strange places. They were like some of those places you read of in books – the old people were full of superstitions and the Islands were full of old legends and stories. Here and there on the Island were big mounds of ground and, according to the stories, these were old tombs etc. of old Kings and people from some bygone century. Also, there were old stoneworks similar to the Stonehenge of England.

There was also the legendary ghosts here and there – and one of the boys was supposed to have seen one, coming home one night. Of course, the boys all laughed at him and told him to 'Come off it!' but he was so white and shaken that I was inclined to believe him – if he was fooling, he certainly put on a good act!

21

August–September 1943

After a couple of months on the mainland, the Battalion was then split up on to smaller Islands around Scapa Bay. BHQ stayed in the old camp, but HQ Company and one Rifle Company went over to the Island of Hoy, which overlooked the Navy anchorage. This Island was about 9 miles long by 2 miles wide, but on here was the HQ of the Fleet, a large building and radio station up on a hill, guarded by Royal Marines. Our camp was at the bottom of this hill and lower down the road were all the Naval and Marine camps and training depots.

We had a pretty easy time over on that Island. I was in charge of maintenance of the transport, and so if there was nothing to do I would take a truck and go across to the Company at the other end of the island and see that everything was O.K. As we had nobody important in charge of us, we often went down to the picture show in the Navy camp in the afternoon.

When we needed spares it was a full days job to get over to the mainland. An old trawler ran a ferry service across the bay every hour and from there the Battalion had a truck to meet us and take us to our camp. It was often a pretty rough ride across that bay, which didn't exactly agree with my stomach, but after a few crossings I seemed to stick it a little better. I don't think I was meant to be a sailor or a flyer, my stomach wasn't made for either. However, I can say I tried it, even though it did make me green and bring up my breakfast!

Well, we had about a month of those islands and then we moved back once more to the mainland. This time to a camp about half way between Kirkwall and Stromness. This was a terribly dirty camp, there were no hard paths in the camp and so all round the huts it was ankle deep in mud.

The workshops were not too bad, we had two big sheds complete with pits for repairs, at least we were under cover, which was all we really wanted.

It was pretty quiet at night as usual, nowhere to go, nothing to do to pass the nights away. That was the trouble we had in most of the camps, nothing to pass away the nights. The boredom got us down after months and years like this, and then when the men were 'browned off' with boredom, the trouble always started. Men would overstay leave and morale and spirits would drop. That was what was happening with us, we were so fed-up and depressed we didn't care where we went or what happened, we would have gone abroad anywhere, gladly, just for the change.

Well, we didn't know it at the time, but we were destined for a big change very soon – but, as I said, when it did come we looked forward to the change, no matter what it was. So one day after rumours had been flying around about a move coming off, the CO had a parade of every man in the Hall and told us all the 'gen' we had been waiting for the last few weeks. We were going back to the mainland to start

Lieutenant-Colonel Robert Payton Reid
(Courtesy Robert Sigmond)

training again – but – we were given the honour of joining the famous 1st AIRBORNE DIVISION![1]

Well, when he said that I guess anybody could have wafted all of us down with a feather. As I stood there in that hall I could literally feel the whole crowd sway

---

1   The 1st Airborne Division which had been formed in 1941 consisted of two parachute brigades (1st and 4th) and an airlanding brigade (1st) was in late 1943 in Italy taking part in the campaign there. They had previously taken part in the campaigns in North Africa and Sicily. It was normal for a brigade to have three infantry battalions in it but the 1st Airlanding Brigade in Italy had only two. On formation it had consisted of the 1st Battalion The Border Regiment, the 2nd Battalion The South Staffordshire Regiment and the 2nd Battalion The Oxs and Bucks Light Infantry. This last mentioned unit was removed from the Brigade in early 1943 from North Africa and sent back to the UK to form the nucleus of the 6th Airlanding Brigade, part of the newly forming 6th Airborne Division.

   Just why the 7th KOSB was selected has never been found in any official records but I have a theory which I have discussed with several 7th veterans, all of whom agree with my ideas. I am of the opinion that a Staff Officer either in the War Office or 1st Airborne Corps HQ when looking round for a spare Battalion, came to the conclusion that it would not be proper to break up one of the Divisions earmarked for Operation Overlord. Many of these Divisions had been training for their invasion role for many months, so the options narrowed to a 'home defence unit'. I suspect that any thoughts of the Germans invading the Orkneys and Shetlands in late 1943 had long subsided so a unit from OSDEF was ideal for the 1st Airlanding Brigade.

with surprise. We just looked at each other and mouths opened, but not a word was spoken.

As if to give us heart, the CO had some high ranking Officers there and they gave some nice speeches, telling us how they knew we would uphold the tradition and fighting qualities of that Division. We listened and took it all with a pinch of salt – we'd been in the Army too long to fall for any of that talk! Then they explained to us what had happened to that Division in Sicily when two-thirds of the men were lost in the sea. I guess they must have read our minds, for that is what most of us were thinking about.

Not that we were afraid to go into action, oh! No! The spirit was there alright, but we just wanted to know what our chances were. Very few of us were afraid to go into the fight, so long as we were given a fighting chance against the other guy. We didn't mind having the odds against us on the ground as long as we had a good chance of getting down to the ground. Of course, we knew there would have to be somebody not get down in one piece, but if our chances were, say, 75% or 80% we were quite prepared to take a chance on what came.

So we finally packed up in the Orkneys and were shipped once more to the mainland, this time to dock at Aberdeen. We were once more laden with equipment and trudged through the streets of Aberdeen to a transit camp on the far side. There we had a meal and then sat around in the huts waiting for something to happen.

About tea-time we were again marched across the town to a big Pavilion on the sea front. There we took off equipment and made ourselves comfortable in the seats. We were then given a concert by an Army orchestra – a good one it was, too. Tables were then filled with 'eats' and we had a jolly good tuck in and were quite happy about everything.

Then, about 6.00 pm we again had to 'fall-in' outside on the promenade, where a roll-call was made in the pitch dark. It was not a case of calling the roll to see if anyone was missing. Like a lot more things in the Army, it was just done because it was supposed to be done. It was laid down in King's Regulations that a roll-call should be made, and so we had one.

From there we marched back across the town to the Station, unable to see a thing in the dark, only just able to see the outline of the man in front. We made our way slowly – stop – start – stop – start. Eventually we reached the Station where women of the WVS were giving each one of us a bag containing a haversack ration, which was a good one. We then made ourselves comfortable in the train and got settled down for a night's sleep.

We had a good journey down, but then to crown everything the Adjutant and Sgt. Major came along and told us all that the CO would be waiting for us at the new station and so he told us all to polish up our brasses. Imagine – they couldn't forget blanco and polish for one day! It didn't matter about anything else, just so long as we looked nice and pretty. That was just typical of the Army, and especially of our Battalion, all through the war and even to the time we eventually went into action with the Liberation Armies.

So we eventually reached our destination, where we were formed up outside on the country road and then – with the Pipe Band in front making enough noise to awaken the dead – we marched down the road to the village where our camps were. This was about 7.00 am so as could be imagined, bedroom windows were thrown open and curious heads peaked out, wondering what on earth could be making such a noise as those bagpipes and still live!

22

November 1943–August 1944

Woodhall Spa, Lincolnshire

1st Airlanding Brigade (1st Airborne Division)

Such was our entry into our new station, Woodhall Spa. A quiet, little residential place, or rather had been, pre-war, for now there was a Battalion of the Border Regiment in huts just behind the main road. Also, about ½ mile up the road there were two more Battalions – first, the South Staffs. Regt. and then us, the KOSB's, so that from then on the little village was always busy with troops and traffic.

There was nothing in the village for entertainment, apart from a very small, makeshift Cinema (which I never even saw), and three pubs, so that we spent most of our time either at Lincoln or Boston, which were 20 miles in opposite directions.

For the first few weeks we were on our own, because the other Battalions had not yet landed from Italy, and the fact that we were Airborne was a secret. We still wore our khaki berets and it was impressed on us that we were not to mention the

L/Cpl. Albert Blockwell. Albert aged 23
(Editor's collection)

61

fact to anybody. This was to keep the movement of the Airborne Division from Italy a secret from the Germans.

So for those first weeks we did practically nothing – we had no transport, except for half a dozen 3 tonners. So that us in the MT had a hard job filling the day in doing nothing, for if we admitted we had nothing to do, we would have had to do drill parades with the other lads, so we managed to scrounge away the time.

Then a programme was laid down for each day, and this included PT twice every morning and then sport every afternoon. For us in the MT this afternoon sport usually consisted of a road run. The Rifle Companies usually had a cross-country run or football matches. We always had it easier than the Rifle Companies, for after all, we still did our marching in trucks! We had what is known in the Army as 'petrol feet', although we had to be physically fit to be able to do any marching or anything else if we were called upon to do it.

I might add, we were capable of holding our own at marching and shooting with any of the other lads, as we often proved it —for often on the range we came up pretty high in points for shooting. We were fortunate to have six or seven good shots in the MT, myself included. However, personally I was not consistent at shooting, which meant some days I was good and the next I would be off, although I was always able to put up a good show, on or off.

We took to the PT and runs pretty hard at first, but after a while we began to enjoy them. After dinner we would set off through the woods and across the moorland where we would come onto the main road. Then we would set off at a steady run down the road and circle round about 8 miles and then back to camp where we

My sweetheart, 'Dorothy'
(Editor's collection)

My girl. LACW Dorothy Newton 2095310
(Editor's collection)

would have a good shower and rub down. Yes! We must have been fit alright, when I think of the way we used to trot along those roads, mile after mile.

At night we often walked into Horncastle, a small town about 4 miles away, where we could go to a Picture House and Canteen and have a drink and then walk back. We often went there those first weeks.

We then had stiff medical tests. We had to be perfectly fit for Airborne troops, for with perfect fitness came stamina, and that is what we had to have – to be able to keep going without sleep or food with heavy equipment, after the others had stopped. A good many of the boys failed in these medicals, the low grade men were posted back to Depot and those who were not quite up to the mark were put into the Administration and Seaborne Companies.[1] These Companies were to go across by sea and then contact us on the other side, with stores and clothing etc.

---

1   Unlike the parachute element of the Division the gliderborne elements did not have to volunteer to be 'airborne' but there was still a selection process, even if the men were unaware of it. In D Company this is what happened as the CSM WO2 J Swanston recalls: 'A weeding-out process started and for my own Company this process turned out to be satisfactory. The method was an easy one. I marched the men one by one to the Medical Officer. I was to stand just behind the man to be examined and then I would just nod yes or no to the doctor. This resulting in a positive or negative check. I am sure some never understood why they were turned down.'

Mum, 'Eva' (Editor's collection)

I passed A.1 and as it turned out I was the only one of the Fitters to fly at all. The others, Bill Eaves, Bill Kerr and Sergeant Fuller all went over by sea, later on. So I was, as I jokingly used to say to the boys, 'Joe Soap, the Flying Fitter!'

Well, Christmas was now drawing close and rumours of leave, so we were feeling quite happy. The Battalion was to go in two parts, some at Christmas, the rest at New Year. I arranged for mine at New Year for my girl was taking hers then. She was then in the WAAFs, I had met her whilst on leave from the Orkneys and had corresponded regularly ever since. In fact, although she did not know it or believe it, she was my real girl from then on and I meant to keep her.

We had a jolly good 'tuck in' that Christmas – Christmas dinner, beer, cigarettes, all served by the Officers. Then for the rest of the week we were in Boston every night and what a week that was! The people of Boston were good-hearted and it was the liveliest little town I'd ever been in, and there was the finest Canteen there I'd ever been in. The 'Fighting Forces Canteen' was the name and was run by the WVS. It was clean and the suppers of chips, sausage, peas etc. were just done fine and cheap too – every soldier who ever visited Boston knew the 'Fighting Forces Canteen'.

Then came New Year and our leave. We were still on the 'secret list' so that on the train we still had to wear our old khaki berets, until we got home. I don't think Mum and Dad were very pleased to see me in that Red Beret, but they didn't say anything, I guess they were just a bit worried.

I had my leave and had New Year's Eve with Dorothy. I remember leaving our house and Mum hoped I would be home for the next one. Well! I had my own feelings of what was to come that year and I wondered to myself, "Would I be here to see the next New Year?" Little did any of us know what we were to go through and who were going to see it through O.K.

Dad, 'Albert' (Editor's collection)

Well, we eventually got back to camp and then began training in earnest. We began to get fully equipped with new weapons, new trucks, etc., and we were kept busy for weeks travelling to different parts of the country for trucks, motorbikes, etc. We collected 70 lightweight motorbikes from Peterborough and 70 heavy motorbikes from Birmingham. In the meantime, drivers collected trucks and Jeeps from other places, so finally, after a few weeks, we were up to full strength in transport. Eventually we got our full equipment too, radio sets, small arms, medical supplies and extra equipment that we had to carry.

At this time, the country had a big job on equipping fighting units abroad, and so it can be imagined how difficult it was to supply and build up an Airborne Army and at the same time fulfil their commitments abroad. Therefore, all through our training we were always just that little bit short. If we had smashes or needed replacements, well, they just weren't there.

It was the same with the flying, the Air Force had a terrific programme of bombing to keep to and also the Transport Squadrons, and just weren't numerically strong enough to give us as much flying time as we needed. What was more important, to give the necessary flying time to the Glider Pilots, who were in need of training necessary to have a good reserve of trained pilots.

At the same time, the bombers that were used to tow our Gliders had to be fitted and modified to take towing equipment, so that was another headache, as we just didn't have the number of bombers available to be at the disposal of our Divisions.

So all these elements had to be taken into consideration, for the failure of the Airborne operations that were to come in the following months on the continent.

It was rather a surprise to us to find the heavy load of equipment we now had to carry. We were under the impression that being Airborne we would travel lighter than the normal Infantry. We didn't realise that obviously we would have to carry our own rations and ammunition with us, as we didn't have the transport for ra-

Mortar training
(Copyright: Imperial War Museum H 25882)

tions and light ammunition. When we had our first parade with full equipment, it seemed like a ton weight, but after we got accustomed to it, it didn't seem too bad. As before, modifications were constantly being made to equipment, trying new methods, finding faults, more modifications, and so it went on.

At first we were equipped with the old type lifebelts. These had to be worn around the chest, over the battledress, and were inflated by blowing into a tube. Underneath our battledress we wore a string vest and pullover for warmth when flying, battledress, then lifebelts, then the camouflage smock on top of that. In the large pockets of the smock we had in No. 1, two shell dressings, in No. 2, two Mill's bombs, in No. 3, dubbin and brushes for boots and in No. 4, our Red Beret. Round our neck we wore a large camouflage net for a scarf and a yellow identity silk square.

Then came our equipment, in one pouch I carried a smoke grenade, an electric torch and a hand grenade (Mill's bomb), and in the other, 70 rounds of .303 ammunition and an iron ration (chocolate). Fastened to the back of the equipment was an anti-tank mine, round my chest were two more bandoliers of ammunition, then in the small pack on my back there were two 24 hour rations and a change of socks, towel, toiletries etc. On my back also there was an entrenching tool (small shovel) and a water bottle. Last, but not least was, of course, a rifle.

So that was me fully loaded, what we called 'light and mobile' but, as I said before, we were light compared to some of the other lads. The Signal boys, for in-

Glider training
(Copyright: Imperial War Museum H 26172)

stance, had all that and a radio set and spare batteries as well. So there was no doubt about it, we had to be tough, or crazy to do it – I think there was a bit of both!

Well, we then started training for our new role. In the field near the camp there was a Glider fuselage, and in this we practiced loading and unloading Jeeps and trailers. This was a labourious job, needing 6 or 8 men to lift the Jeep round inch by inch, to get it in and out the door at the side. Of course, in action we loosed off the tail of the Glider and drove out this way, but this could not be done in training.

Then, once inside, the Jeeps and trailers had to be lashed down with numerous chains and shackles. This job often took about 4 hours of hot, awkward work, squeezing along the sides, underneath and climbing over the top. When a Jeep was in a Glider it was a dead fit for size, only allowing a few inches to spare at each side, so it can be imagined how awkward it was to fit chains, etc., just where they had to be. It was important that these chains be fitted correctly and to the correct points – blocks were fitted under chassis too, so that there was no 'give' on the springs. Everything just had to be perfect and no 'slip ups', for if anything came loose 'upstairs', we had 'had it', for the sides of those Gliders were only thin plywood and would stand no hard knocks. When loading the Jeeps, steel plates were used in the doorway to slide the Jeep on and then troughs were placed along the inside, for the wheels to fit into, otherwise the wheels and everything would have broken clean through the bottom. When on the road, these long steel troughs had to be chained to either side of the Jeep and utilized for crossing ditches, etc.

Those Jeeps certainly took some punishment too, for they, like us, were loaded to full capacity. We were kept busy for weeks making modifications to those Jeeps to adapt them for Airborne. Steering wheels had to be easily removable, carriers for shells, etc. had to be fitted on bonnets and wings, carriers for stretchers fitted, and wings cut to pass the door of the Glider. Those Jeeps were the most useful and adaptable trucks produced in the War without a doubt. For everyday use they were used as a 4 seater with windscreen and canopy, and then for active service the windscreens and canopies were removed and each one would be loaded for it's respective job.

All of them towed either one or two trailers, and the Anti-Tank Platoon towed the 6 pounder guns, others were fitted for heavy machine guns. The Anti-Tank Jeeps were the most heavily laden – on the bonnet they carried six heavy shells and three on the front bumper, four or five men, two often riding on the gun itself to stop it bouncing. Then those heavy steel troughs were chained on either side and then there was all the usual equipment besides, camouflage nets, petrol tins, tools, men's rifles and equipment and sleeping bags. We all carried those sleeping bags with us during training, they were good things and I always maintained that those bags were the best equipment they ever gave us.

We began many exercises again, travelling all over the country to do them, Yorkshire Moors, Salisbury Plains, even as far south as Poole Bay. We often spent weeks away from camp on those exercises. Of course, most of those exercises were with the rest of the Division, including the Parachute Battalions and so big areas were needed for them and for dropping supplies. Our camp at Woodhall was next to a RAF bomber 'drome, but none of these 'dromes were equipped with Gliders. So for all flying we had to go down to Salisbury and Swindon area where most of the 'dromes were Transport Command and it was on all those 'dromes that the Gliders were.

Airborne training
(Copyright: Imperial War Museum CH 12965)

Exercises now were quite different from what we had been doing, they were well organised, we knew where we were going and what our job was. Also, we carried our own rations and were able to brew our own tea on the small 'Tommy' cookers we had. In most of our Jeeps we carried portable cookers, so that they were handy for the 'brew', and as could be imagined, whenever we stopped for a few minutes there was always someone who would have a 'brew' going. Often we would light up and get a dixie on (we carried tins of water in each Jeep) and then just as we were coaxing the water to boil we would have to move. This was so regular that we knew when we were going to move on, just when the water was nice and hot!

The people were very good to us too. Whenever we halted near any houses, the people never failed to come out with tea and cakes for us. I guess they all looked up to us lads with the Red Berets, as if we were something out of the ordinary, for they always gave us all they could spare. I know that, for more than once a lady would come out of a house and hand us a few cakes, and say sort of apologetically, "I'm afraid that's all I have for you".

Yes! We had some good times travelling about the country and we often looked forward to them. Those Jeeps were not exactly luxurious neither, for with no windscreens the wind and rain just cut us in half from the 'tummy' up. We often had a good laugh though, for the boys would have gas-capes on when the weather was bad. Then in all the Jeeps we carried two blankets for the stretchers, and the boys would wrap these all round them, shoulders and everything, so that all that could be seen was a great bundle of blanket and two heads with Red Berets on top! No wonder the people laughed as we passed through the towns, but we didn't care

Airlanding troops with handcart
(Copyright: Imperial War Museum H 25880)

for nothing – that was the spirit that was wanted and that was the spirit we had. We took everything with a laugh and a joke, and we always laughed at somebody else's misfortune, but tried to help them if we could, at the same time.

23

March 1944

About the beginning of March, Bill Kerr and I had to go on a Diesel Course to Ashton-under-Lyme, near Manchester. We looked forward to a course like this, for we thought it would be in or near a town and so we had visions of good times in Manchester. I was pleased to go on that course too, for it was at my trade and I was always learning and would benefit myself by it.

Well, we set off one day for Ashton, with kit and kitbag as usual, but now we had got wise to these courses and only took our bare necessities and left the rest in the care of the boys. It was an awkward place to get to by train, but we didn't mind. We broke the journey at Manchester and had a good dinner in the YMCA Canteen. We eventually arrived at the Barracks about teatime and went through the usual routine of 'checking in' etc.

The following morning we started the Course, this wasn't so good because reveille was at 6.00 am and we were in the classes by 7.15 am which was a little early for us, but the classes were very interesting.

As could be imagined, we had good nights in the town. Ashton was a lively town alright, crowded with girls, and the people were as good as their reputation had been. We only had to walk into a pub and drinks would come up for us right away and then somebody would offer cigarettes and start conversation and more often than not we would be invited home for supper. Yes! Those people were the most homely and hospitable I have ever mixed amongst – maybe it was the Red Beret again, I don't know. Anyway, we had a good time and were sorry to leave.

About the second day I was there I was going up to the NAAFI when I saw a face that was familiar to me. I looked again. Yes, it was! Ken Smith, who had left us 2½ years ago. He had Corporal's stripes and the Africa Star ribbon. Yes! Since leaving us he had been to the desert, took part in the invasion of Italy and then home again. He was a changed man from the one who went away in 1941 – in those days he was very quiet and reserved, and only drank moderately, but now he was out every night and I don't remember seeing him one morning when he was absolutely sober.

I asked him about this change and he told me just what I kind of expected. He said, "It was when I was on that beach-head and faced sudden death. I got to thinking how quiet I had lived, and when I listened to the other lads talking and laughing about the good nights they had experienced in different places, I got to thinking about life, and I sort of made up my mind. I promised himself if ever I get out of this alive and get home, I'm going to enjoy myself and have a good time before I come out again". So there he was, and he was doing just that – wine, women and song every night!

That just typified what most of us felt and thought in those days, especially when we knew that we were certain to be in the battles to come. I, myself, and most of my mates were the same. We were in a fighting mob and we didn't know just what was to come sooner or later, so we went out and enjoyed ourselves and had a good time while it lasted.

Well, the course eventually finished and we went back to Woodhall. We arrived back in the afternoon and went straight to the office to see about leave. They then told us we could only have 5 days as everyone had to be back from leave by 1st April. We didn't know what to make of that – was the invasion to start then? We didn't know – anyway we took what we could and that night we were home on leave.

However, I didn't have long at home for the following morning we were recalled and I met Bill on Doncaster station. We had to wait all that day for connections and finally got back to camp late that night to find everybody had moved. Only a rear party was left, so we managed to find a bit of our kit and after getting 'railroaded' by the CSM who put us on a charge we set off by train with the rear party for somewhere down south.

24

April 1944

We arrived at our new camp the following morning, a place we were to visit frequently in the coming months. We found the MT boys and got ourselves a bed and found the rest of our kit and then started asking what all the panic was about. As usual, it was nothing at all, just an exercise.[1]

We were in front of the CO the following morning and charged with being absent – we were left off with 2 days pay stopped (we expected being stripped).

The camp was called Bulford – it was a big area of camps and training grounds, near to Tidworth. The camp was pretty good, a good canteen, but not much entertainment. There were two Cinemas in the main camp, but at night we wanted to get away from military and khaki, so as usual, we sneaked out with trucks at night to Andover or somewhere like that and had some good 'booze ups'.

Amesbury was a small town about 20 minutes walk across the fields – we often went there at nights. We soon got to know our way around, found the best canteens, etc., and spent most of our time slipping out in trucks visiting them. Every morning about 10.00 am we would go up the road to a little shack on the corner of the main road – 'Jock's Café' was the name – and he made smashing bacon rolls in the morning, so that was where we often had our breakfast.

We were then kitted for the exercise, lifebelts, rations etc., and then had to load up Gliders with Jeeps etc. The 'drome was miles away, at Brize Norton, and we were transported there by RASC.

This was the first time most of us had seen the Gliders taking off and it wasn't very encouraging or pleasing to watch. We were all in Glider loads of 27 – I was flying with 'B' Company, and then had to contact an MT Jeep, if possible.

We stood on the 'drome and watched the first of the Gliders take off – it was a slow job. A tractor would tow the Glider up behind the bomber, an old Stirling, and ground crew would connect the tow rope. Then at a signal, away they went. The Glider was airborne in a hundred yards or so and for the rest of the run was tearing along behind the bomber about 20 feet up in the air. In the meantime, it was tilting from side to side, just missing the ground, going up and down, until the pilot got the 'feel' of it. It was absolutely hair-raising to watch, to say the least!

After seeing those first ones take off, I could hardly realise that it was our turn next. However, there was no backing out, we had to go – at least, we could back

---

1   Around March and April 1944 the Battalion was kept very busy, on 14th March General Sir Bernard Montgomery visited the Brigade. From the bonnet of a Jeep he addressed the assembled troops and it was stated he made everyone feel a part of his invasion Army and part of a force that would end the War. Two days later King George VI accompanied by Lieutenant-General Browning, the GOC of the Division Major- General Urquhart and Brigade Commander Brigadier Hicks inspected the Battalion. From the end of March until early April the unit took part in Exercise Boomerang based at Bulford Camp in Wiltshire.

Princess Alice inspecting 7th KOSB 1944
(Copyright: Imperial War Museum H 36044)

out, as some did, but not me. I was more scared of the disgrace than of the Gliders! Anyway, like all other times, if the boys were going, I was game to go with them.

So we climbed in, fastened straps, held our breath and said a silent prayer, at least, I think I did. The roar of the four engines of the bomber rose louder and louder, until the Glider shuddered and vibrated in the wind. Then, with a jerk, we were moving – faster – and faster! We tore down that runway, then we lifted and like the others, slipped from left to right. I could see the green fields flying past the wing – 160 mph! I looked at the bomber, it was still tearing along, and I said under my breath, "Come on, old pal, get her up" and then we were both airborne and well off the ground.

I experienced all that every time I took off – no wonder we had to have good hearts. I often listened to mine after we were off the ground, it was going like a trip-hammer. The tension didn't cease until we were about 1,000 feet up, for anywhere under that level, if anything happened to the bomber, we wouldn't have had a chance to land ourselves. I often pictured what would happen if we hit the ground whilst taking off. We would be dragged along the ground at 100 mph, breaking to pieces – that was my greatest fear and dread. Once we were on our own we could slow down and if necessary hit the ground at a much slower speed and on wheels at that.

Well, we climbed steadily and then made for our route, which was over Bath and then South to the Channel and along to Southampton and then up over Winchester and back to Brize Norton. After about half an hour's flying we ran into very bad weather, clouds and mist. I don't know whether our 'tug' flew 'over' the

Princess Alice inspecting 7th KOSB 1944
(Copyright: Imperial War Museum H 36050)

weather or by luck we missed the worst of it. Anyway, we completed the route alright, at least the 'planes did, but not my stomach – I was feeling awfully sick.

Those bombers or Gliders seem to fly lovely and smoothly from the ground, but that is far from correct. All the time they are swaying up and down, up and down, all the time, worse than any ship could ever toss, and so my stomach was like before, on the ship, making some queer convulsions. I was lucky, though, as the next seat to me was vacant so that I was able to lay down a bit, then I could 'take it' alright. However, just before 'casting off' we had to strap in again and for about 5 minutes I had a job to keep my stomach down.

We touched down and made a perfect landing in the darkness and out we tumbled. I jumped to the ground and vomited my heart up! The boys laughed at me. I just laughed back. I didn't give a hoot.

Gliders were swishing in from all directions, some crashing into others, but none fatal. We had to keep on the lookout for other Gliders coming in and be ready to duck.

Just before we 'cast off', I looked down to the ground and the darkness was closing in. I could see the field landing lights on – what a small field! Surely we didn't have to land in that small space? I looked the other way, darkness all round, I had a twinge of fear touch me, we seemed so alone and fragile up in that darkness. The roar of the bomber and tearing of the wind seemed to exaggerate everything. It was as if some roaring monster was trying to close in on us – that's the best way I could explain that feeling.

Princess Alice inspecting 7th KOSB 1944
(Copyright: Imperial War Museum H 36049)

Well, we formed up in small sections and then made for predetermined check points, etc. I started marching with that section in the dark and expected meeting up with some transport, but not me! I was marching for the rest of the night!

We hadn't marched for more than a few minutes before we were soaked in sweat. All that equipment plus the lifebelt was too warm for marching. The trouble was, we had to put on pullovers for warmth when flying, for it was below zero up there at times, and then on the ground we didn't have time to take anything off, so we just had to sweat and like it.

The exercise was rather a flop for us, for all the Companies marched off the field and left Jeeps etc. in the Gliders. It was impossible for two men to unload alone, so some of the lads had to go back again. A check up was then made by radio to all Companies and it was then found we were 7 Gliders missing.

About 2.00 am the exercise was then called off, which pleased us alright, and we were lucky, for RASC trucks were near to us at the time, so we piled in and were away. When I walked in the billet, the other lads (who weren't on the exercise) looked at me and asked me if we landed O.K. I said, "Yes, we got down O.K."

Then they told me that trucks had to go out all over to pick up those men who had come down, but one Glider was known to have crashed with a full load of men. Every man was killed in that crash, 27 of them, and so we didn't know which one it was that had crashed, as all the other Gliders that had come down were not yet checked. So we sat up and waited for the boys all coming in – our boys were O.K. – they all came in, so it was one of the Company Gliders. We never did find out what exactly happened in that crash. It was my opinion that it had been towing when it hit the ground, for everything was smashed to pieces. They didn't tell us a thing about it or how it happened – for us it was best forgotten.[2]

2　The accident referred to here took place on 4th April 1944. The 7th KOSB were due to take place in a navigational exercise called Dreme. They were to be towed by Short Stirlings of 196 and 299 Squadrons from RAF Keevil on a cross country flight before the gliders would land on the runways at RAF Brize Norton. Once on the ground the exercise would continue. Number 3 Platoon of A Company were in Horsa LG999 piloted by Staff Sergeant H Joel and Sergeant W Walker, and during the flight somewhere near Romsey and Winchester the towing aircraft crashed. This caused the Horsa to also crash and all the occupants were killed- Lieutenant Eastman the OC of 3 Platoon and 25 of his men and the two pilots.

25

May–June 1944

Well, we settled down again in Bulford for a few weeks, occasionally going to a 'drome trying some new methods out and for a bit of flying. From the camp we could see a Parachute training area and we often stood and watched them for hours. Those Transport flyers were pretty good on night exercises. They often flew over us as if dropping supplies and there would often be 50 'planes in perfect formation in the dark, with lights on – it looked a wonderful sight, all those red and green lights in the dark sky.

We eventually went back to our home camp, Woodhall, and were then busy for weeks making repairs. On all those convoys there was always someone who had a smash or turned over a trailer or two. When a Jeep was towing two trailers, the maximum speed possible was only about 20 mph, otherwise the rear trailer began to 'snake' and would turn over, and this often happened.

Whenever we moved in convoy, there was always 3 or 4 different ones, first the heavy trucks would go together, then Jeeps and Anti-Tank guns, then Jeeps and single trailers, then the double trailers. Often on those convoys we would have some stupid Officer with us who couldn't read a map and we would be lost for hours while he found out where we were. I remember on one convoy down to Bulford, an Officer in the lead took us the wrong road and we all finished up in a ploughed field!

I wouldn't care, but most of us MT lads knew the way down to Salisbury without a map. Of course, in those days there were no signposts anywhere, which made travelling difficult, but we knew most of those routes by memory. Another thing was, nearly all those convoys always went by a different route. I suppose this was for propaganda reasons, so that it would look as if there were thousands of us Airborne troops, when all the time it was the same units going down another route.

Well, we started the old routine once more – Boston every night. All the time we were at Woodhall I don't remember one night when some trucks weren't out to Boston, mostly unofficially, it was amazing we weren't caught. At night we would get ready and in two's and three's make our way over to the trucks, and then in we would get and away, passing Police and Officers, and holding our breath in case they stopped us for a work ticket, but never once was I caught. The Regimental Police tried many times to catch us, but we always got to know and would take a different road. Yes! We took hundreds of chances those nights, and got away with them. If we had stayed in camp and not had good nights like that, what a miserable time we would have had.

It was the same in the mornings, we were not allowed cakes for break at 10.00 am, but that didn't stop us. Every morning we would go into Woodhall and have tea and cakes at a small café there. Often, if the Police were down there we would go to Horncastle to the canteen there. Usually, though, the Police lads didn't say anything to us, for we often gave them lifts and us Fitters kept their bikes in good trim, so they were O.K. with us.

We now had exercises pretty regularly, often going up to the Yorkshire Moors and around the Pickering area. We had many exercises up there, spending a week or two on the moors and then back to camp again. We had so many different exercises it is now impossible to remember each one in detail, and so I can't just say when and where we went those months at Woodhall. All I do remember clearly are the nights we nipped away to Boston and Lincoln.

I now had Les Jordan for a mate and we got along O.K. together. He had a small PV truck, as he was the Padre's batman, so we often went out at night in that. Usually we went to Lincoln, for by then the RAF and American Air Force were crowding out Boston and it was too busy. So Lincoln was now our territory at night and we had many good nights there. We often took turns driving, he drove one way, I the other, but I don't expect it would have made much difference. If we had been caught, we would have both got the same time 'over the wall'.

On some of the exercises too we often took a truck or motorbike out and went home for a night. I went home a few times like this – had my girl, Dorothy, been at home, I would have gone more often, but as it was I didn't take too many chances. Even so, we took a chance anytime we went home on those motorbikes. With the petrol we used in those days it was quite common for the valves to 'seize up' about every 50 miles or so – so that I always carried a good supply of tools with me.

We were pretty safe from 'Redcaps', for we had our camouflage kit and equipment on and they could see we were on an exercise. Also, we often carried a fake work ticket made out for 'Exercise Snowball' or something like that. We were not obliged to say where we were from or where our camp was, our moves were secret even to the 'Redcaps', but I was always lucky, I was never once stopped or asked questions. Lady Luck always seemed to ride or fly with me.

Once more we went down south for flying exercises. This time we were more fortunate, the weather was good and we had no accidents. I was always lucky, for never once did the rope break or did I make a bad landing. Those tow-ropes often broke if there was a bad Pilot either in the 'tug' or the Glider, and then the Glider Pilot had to look for a place to set down. When those things were fully loaded, they didn't glide very far and couldn't fly below about 90 mph, so it was up to the skill of the Pilot to spot a good flat field.

On one big exercise, we were towed by C-47's, known as Dakotas. They were not so powerful and awkward as the Stirlings and we had American Pilots flying us. From then I had a new confidence in the Yank Pilots, for we found they were damn good flyers and often better than our men. Not underrating our men's ability, for as I said before, our lads just didn't get the training that they should have had, but for all that, under fire, I would choose our boys. In a tight corner, as often proved, that old British spirit and guts seemed to come out.

Whilst down there that time we had a pass into Reading and had a good weekend there.

Once more we went back to Woodhall and back to exercises and work. We managed to get another leave in, and once more we had the 'needle', this time we were inoculated for active service, anti-tetanus, etc., so we knew something was coming sooner or later, as could be expected.

One morning, as we came back from breakfast, we heard the news on the radio. That morning our forces had landed from air and sea on the coast of Normandy, France – the big show was on!

From then on our life was sort of changed, we didn't know when our day was to come, and orders were made and changed from day to day. One day we would be given orders to 'stand-to' and the next we would be 'stood-down'. So we were constantly kept on our toes, a sort of excitement, or tension seemed to be with us all the time. Like everyone else, we read and listened to the news every day, discussing the fighting, and giving our opinions about the moves to come.

We often knew when a move was likely, for we would be given orders to get all repairs completed for a certain date, and so we could count on a move coming. Also, we would be issued with rations, etc., so there were dozens of small things that gave us an inkling of something coming off. Things didn't change at all for us, we just carried on with the usual Battalion or Brigade exercises and having a good time at nights.

26

July 1944

About July, we again went up to the Yorkshire Moors for another big exercise and firing on the ranges. Up the usual route, through Goole, Selby, and halted the first night around the Pickering area. We didn't get much rest – as usual, we moved in the dark and took up positions against the Parachute Battalions. Our Companies were 'fighting' most of the time. After a couple of days we had a rest and we drew into the grounds of a Private Children's Hospital. I remember us looking through field glasses every time a nurse showed up!

We were kept busy there, as we had a truck and motorbikes broken down. From there, one day, Jim Fuller and I went through to Stockton to the REME Workshop for spares, and of course, called home. Then back to York for more spares, and then back to Helmsley where the Battalion was resting. We needed papers signing, so back again we went to York and got our spares. This time we had Bill Eaves with us and we called at a small country pub on the way back and so it was very late and dark when we finally got back again to camp. The Battalion moved on again the following day and left us with plenty of rations etc. and then we followed up when we got the repairs finished.

On most of those exercises, incidentally, we were not allowed bread and were supposed to live on biscuits and hardtack. So it was a daily job for us to do a round of the shops nearby and get in a supply of bread – we always managed to keep a few loaves in stock. We were lucky, for on all convoys we always travelled in the rear and so were able to stop at shops for bread and cigarettes whenever we wanted. Another tiresome job on convoys was riding the motorbikes, for all day long as we rode up and down the line of Jeeps there was always someone wanting cigarettes. First one, then another, would give us money until we had money everywhere. Then, after doing the shopping we would ride past and throw cigarettes and change into the Jeep as we went by.

We often had to put up with bad weather, usually soaking wet all day long, but it was the kind of life I enjoyed – always on the move, seeing different places, never knowing what tomorrow would bring, or where we would go to.

One exercise I remember we had on the Yorkshire Moors – we were up on 'live' firing, the Battalions were in positions on the Moors. At first Bill Eaves was up in front with them, and we were a few miles back taking things easy. Then he came back and I went up – it was the roughest ride I'd ever had. I set off along the rough tracks, through woodland, struggling with the heavy bike all the way. I came to a small HQ etc., asked the way to the KOSB's, rode across more wicked, rough country, then out on top of the Moors. I passed the artillery, all 'dug in' and I knew the infantry boys would be well in front. On across miles of barren moorland – by now my legs were sore and my behind too! I came to the Border Regiment, they were in Reserve – on further where I could see a few Jeeps half 'dug in'. I eventually reached them and found two of the drivers squatting down, as usual, trying to get a 'brew' going.

I stayed with them for the rest of the day and then that night we were to move across to some other valley, miles away. The Company lads had a tough march, right over a range of hills, all night. The transport had to go back and round by road about 10 miles. In the dark we formed up, and as it happened I got mixed up with the Bren Carriers, and it can be imagined what a dust those things caused. I couldn't see the dark ground very well with goggles on, so I just had to squint my eyes and struggle along in the dark. Once I started going I dared not stop, for other stuff was right behind me and we had no lights, so I didn't relish the idea of a Carrier climbing up my back. So I just had to keep on going. We finally got onto the road and then we speeded up and at dawn we sorted ourselves out, in our own Battalions, etc.

We reached our new place and the Gunners were already stripped to the waist, digging pits for the big Anti-Tank guns, what a job! I felt sorry for those lads. We had breakfast and then the transport moved back into a big field, where we rested and tried to have a nap. My eyes were terrible, aching and sore and watering all the time – I suffered for that night ride.

The next trouble was the flies, gnats, mosquitoes, etc. – they gathered round in swarms, as was the same on all those exercises in the summer. We tied scarves around our faces and necks, sat over smoking fires, anything to try to drive away those flies, but no! The flies stuck out the smoke, just to get at us and bite and itch, we were nearly driven mad with them.

It was a glorious day, that day, the sun just blazed away all day long and it was really lovely up there on those Moors and I enjoyed it alright. I could have stayed there a week – doing nothing!

That night we were to go back, in the dark. We began to move off, this time for Scarborough – just the job! I knew my way round those roads alright, I told two of the drivers to follow me. I went up the road to miss the convoy and down Blue Bank and then bypassed Whitby and on to Scarborough.

We stayed in Scarborough that July for three smashing weeks. We were billeted in requisitioned hotels and boarding houses all along the North Cliff. I shared a small front room with Johnny McGurk. It was really good there those few weeks. We got up in the morning and looked out over the sea and watched holidaymakers bathing – we shivered!

We had a good workshop in a garage, and every night we were out along the front, over South Cliff amongst the amusements. Weekends, we strolled around the park and laid up on the cliffs, we were enjoying life.

We had another exercise there, once more onto the Moors. It was on this exercise that Bill Woods 'bogged' his Jeep, way over near Guisbrough. We were all back in billets and the Sergeant came for me and asked me if I wanted to go and find him, as I knew my way around those Moors. Sure! I would go! I set off with a map and a general idea of where he was. I toured over those Moors for hours before I accidentally found them in a valley, the Jeep well down in a bog. I couldn't do anything so I told them to climb in my Jeep and we would go for a breakdown truck to … Stockton! – We stayed at home overnight!

Then in the morning we went round to the REME Workshop for a breakdown truck. The ATS were all for us, gave us eggs for breakfast, and then they followed us out to the Moors. We managed to 'bog' the breakdown truck, but finally pulled out the Jeep with the winch. We arrived back at billets O.K., after calling at Whitby for a snack. The boys looked at me when I told them I had to go to Stockton for a breakdown truck … and laughed!

We settled down once more, having a couple of days off duty, after the exercise. We could have stayed there all summer, we certainly had a good holiday there!

We had three good weeks at Scarborough, with no rumours of moving at all, and then one morning at Reveille we were told to have our kit-bags packed and outside by 9.00 am and be all lined up to move at 10.00 am – what a surprise for us! However, we were quite used to the moves by then, so that any quick move was sort of expected from day to day, but usually we got a bit of 'gen' about a move coming. In Airborne, though, all moves were 'Top Secret' and just as well too, for if we could get to know all about movements, etc., so could Jerry and we didn't want any reception committee when we went over.

We were now in the 21st Army Group, which was the Invasion Army, and so we (the Battalion) were in constant communication with Airborne HQ. Our CO was constantly away for days at a time at conferences, and when we saw him coming back to camp, we usually expected something coming off, either an operation or an exercise.

These exercises often took place in an area similar to an area in France or somewhere like that. So when we heard a rumour of an 'op' coming, or rather a 'Flap' as we called them, we looked at maps of the continent and compared a recent exercise with areas in France and we often got an idea of where we might 'drop in'.

A definite clue we got to a 'Flap' was knowing the Intelligence Officer (IO) was going to Gainsborough for maps, so that when the driver came back with him we would all pounce on him and see if he knew what maps he had got – what country, etc.

27

July–August 1944, Keevil

Well, we arrived back at camp, but we didn't stop long, we were away the next morning and down to the 'drome, this time to Keevil, where we loaded Gliders and then were 'sealed' in the tented camp nearby. We were 'briefed', shown maps, landing zones (LZ) and objectives, etc. Everybody had to memorise the area, landmarks, etc., roads, where to make for, who to shoot on sight and who were French partisans – we seemed to know everything.

Our first operation was to be Caen[1], where the landing was held up. We were 'kitted out', told our 'zero hour' and then usually the Padre gave us a service in the camp. The night came, we laid in the tents, talking, smoking, jumpy and feeling a queer emptiness in our stomachs. We didn't sleep much, we were full of thoughts – what would it be like? – would we make it? A 101 different things we thought about. Then, during the night, someone came round the tents – 'op' cancelled! Our feelings could be imagined! It seemed like Jerry had moved two Panzer Divisions onto the area we were to land – good for us we didn't go, Lady Luck was still with me! That made us think a bit – had Jerry got to know our move, or was it a coincidence – we wondered!

Well, that was the start of many such 'Flaps' that were cancelled just on 'zero hour'. Sometimes we unloaded the Gliders, sometimes they were left on the 'drome, for often an alternative 'Flap' would be on, in a few days time, and this too would subsequently be cancelled.

Sometimes, after a cancelled operation, we would go back to Woodhall and then be given a short leave, with the result that we had four or five leaves in as many months. We didn't stay long at camp before another operation would be on – the same all over again. Load up Gliders, 'briefing', sealed camp and then cancelled.

We then spent a great deal of our time down south, so that we were there handy in case of an operation. In the camp next to ours at Bulford there were Polish Paratroops and in the next one still, Canadian Paratroops, so it was pretty crowded down there. We often went along to their canteen and had a chat with them.

It was a funny thing, we always thought parachuting was a dead loss and too dangerous – and yet most of those Paratroops said we were crazy to fly in Gliders. Most of them admitted they wouldn't fly in those things, in fact, some were known to refuse to fly in them. I suppose it was a matter of confidence, the Parachute boys had never gone up without a 'chute on and had no fear of anything happening to the 'planes, and so the idea of flying without a 'chute sort of took away that confi-

---

1 Regretfully it would seem Albert was slightly confused here as the Operation planned for the Caen area was actually planned for June. The 7th KOSB was briefed by the CO on 11th June and the Operation was called Wild Oats. The next day it was postponed for 24 hours, then again twice for a further 24 hours each time. Eventually the plan was put on hold for 48 hours before it was cancelled for good. This was just the start of many such schemes which involved everyone in many briefings and loading and unloading of gliders as we shall see.

dence. With us, it was different, we had always flown without 'chutes and we had to have confidence in Pilots and Gliders, otherwise we never would have gone up.

I, myself, never had perfect confidence in those Gliders, although I flew in them. I always sort of half-expected something to happen, a wing or rudder to break off or something like that. Most of the other boys were the same, so if anything had happened, I certainly wouldn't have been surprised. Whenever I climbed in them, I just resigned myself to fate and good luck, like most of the other fellows did, and hoped for the best.

Now, when I look back and think of those days, I think I must have been crazy – or else I had a whole lot of courage. I don't think it was courage, for I was often scared stiff, but for all that, I never hesitated and was always calm outwardly.

Had I wanted, I could have been taken off flying for I was always sick, but had I done that it would have meant Bill Eaves going in my place. As he was married and had a family I just didn't feel like backing out. Anyway, nobody likes the idea of backing out of anything when the rest of the boys were doing it. There was also that thrill of danger all the time, as if we were defying the old man with the scythe to slice us out of his sky every time we flew. So we experienced that exciting feeling each time we were going up, which the other seaborne lads didn't experience.

28

August 1944

Woodhall

So the weeks passed on, down on the 'dromes, loading or unloading, nights in town in Salisbury or Andover. Back up to Woodhall, nights in Lincoln, the excitement of each day, watching bombers going over in long processions all day long. When we were down south we watched the Dakotas and Gliders going over each morning with supplies and ammunition, watched others loading with petrol and supplies on the 'dromes. Then watched them coming back loaded with wounded, ambulances lined along the length of the runway, taking the boys back to hospital.

On the roads there was the never-ending stream of transport, guns and tanks, day and night, all going in one direction – south, to the Channel ports. American convoys with Yanks on the trucks sitting chewing gum. Yes! Those were exciting days, every day something new to see.

Each day we would read the papers for news and see how the boys were doing. Great things were happening, battles fought, names were idolised and made famous from day to day. We now began to get that feeling of being out of it. Every time we got a 'Flap' on we all felt that exciting tension of going into 'it' and then it would be cancelled. Most of the boys were as pleased as punch when a 'Flap' was cancelled, but I looked at it another way. Each operation was one step nearer Germany every time and as I often said, 'I would rather go now, than be put off time and again and then probably drop inside Germany'.

Also, as each operation advanced, we knew less of the enemy defences, the ground defences, etc., for operations were called on and organised in a matter of a day or so. Therefore the RAF hadn't the time to make a good reconnaissance of the area or take many photographs and also local 'gen' was scarce.

However, as things turned out, we might have gone on one of those 'ops' and then months later we would still have had to drop again farther on. Anyway, I got back O.K. so that I have no grumbles, for I might just as easy have been killed in France, but I think of the thousands of boys who didn't come back, because we were short of men and supplies.

There again, another item was cropping up – Gliders and 'planes. The demand and toll of Gliders and Pilots had been so great in Normandy that we now just didn't have the Gliders, Pilots or 'tug' 'planes to make an Airborne operation of great magnitude. In the invasion of Normandy the number of 'tug' 'planes could not meet the demand needed for one great landing and so it had to be done in two main 'lifts'. As the War progressed, a toll was being taken of those 'planes every day and so by the time we were to go 'over' we suffered the shortage of 'tug' 'planes even more so than the 6th Airborne did.

Also, Dakotas that could have been used for us were urgently needed for maintaining supplies to the far-reaching armoured columns of our main Armies on the ground. So with these things against us we had to finally make our operation

86

against an enemy who was now tightly crowded back into a smaller area and therefore had more fire-power, and also were getting more desperate as we approached their homeland.

29

September 1944

Keevil

We were on another short leave at the time, when suddenly we were recalled back to camp. We thought, 'This is it again!' When we reached Woodhall we found all the seaborne party were loaded up and ready to move. They moved off the following morning and we never saw them again.

We came to two conclusions, either we were going to a base in France or else there was another 'Flap' on – we were all for going to a base in France.[1]

Well, down to Keevil again we went, same thing again, load up, briefing – and then the whole show was cancelled. The morale of the boys was dropping a bit after all those cancellations so we were sent on leave again to cheer us up and then back again to the 'drome.

By now I was kept busy going to different places for spares, for all the MT Stores had gone over by sea and so all I had was some small stuff in one of the Jeeps.

We loaded up once more, this time at a 'drome called Down Ampney. We were briefed for an operation in Holland to seize and hold the Nijmegen Bridge, and once more this was cancelled. We went back to camp again and started count-

---

1   The 1st Airborne Division (or for some operations just a part of it) between June and September were warned of quite a lot of different operations and even today there is controversy about exactly how many operations there were. I will just list the operations stated in the book by Lieutenant Colonel T Otway *Airborne Forces: Second World War, 1939-45 Army* (London, Imperial War Museum, 1990 reprint) who post war was asked to compile the official account of the British Airborne Forces in the Second World War. Issued in 1951 it remained a 'restricted document' till it was reprinted by the Imperial War Museum in 1990 to which interested readers are directed to obtain details of the following operations. Note some were planned (and cancelled) so quickly they never got an official name.
1. Operation Tuxedo
2. Operation Wastage
3. Reinforcement of the US 82nd Airborne Division 7th to 10th June 1944
4. Operation Wild Oats
5. Operation Beneficiary
6. Operation Swordhilt
7. Operation Hands-Up
8. Operation Transfigure
9. Operation Boxer
10. Operation Axehead
11. Operation Linnet
12. Operation Linnet 2
13. Operation Infatuate
14. Operation Comet
15. Operation Market-Garden

Some of the weapons and equipment the Battalion took into action. A 'Flying Flea'
Royal Enfield light motorcycle, against the rear wheel a (long model) 2" Mortar. A Bren
gun next to a Sten gun Mk V and a Lee Enfield rifle. In front of the 6 pounder anti-tank
gun is a No 18 radio set. In front of the Jeep is a 3" Mortar.
(Courtesy Robert Sigmond)

ing the days, as the Gliders were only supposed to stand loaded for 5 days owing to
the strain on the wings. We went the full limit and then had to unload again.

We then moved our camp to the tents near to Down Ampney 'drome and had
yet another 'Flap' – yes, another! Each time we had those operations on, the camp
was sealed and we were not allowed outside the camp, or to communicate with anybody outside, so we were a bit 'browned off'. I guess the CO sensed this, so one afternoon we were all taken to a Picture House in Cirencester, marched inside and
then afterwards straight back into the trucks and back to camp.

Once more our Company (HQ Company) and one Rifle Company went back
to Keevil, the rest of the Battalion was on other 'dromes.

Then came the final operation, this time to a town called Arnhem, in Holland.
We were given Dutch money and once more briefed and shown the aerial photographs of our Landing Zone and our objective.

30

16th–17th September 1944

Arnhem, Holland

The 1st British Airborne Division

Well, this time it seemed pretty definite, our job was to take and hold Arnhem. The bridge over the river was the main objective and we had to hold that until the main ground forces got through to us. When we were briefed, they didn't seem to know about anything definite. We asked about ground defences, flooding etc. They couldn't tell us what it was like at present, we were told it should be O.K. as far as they knew. They knew there was an S.S. Barracks near to where we were landing and that was to be taken care of. Also the RAF were to lay a carpet of bombs between these barracks at Ede and Arnhem. We asked about fighters – the RAF guaranteed us 90% protection – that wasn't too bad neither. How far was 'Monty' away? – 60 miles we were told – that certainly wasn't so good!

That Saturday afternoon we were taken to a tented camp called Broadwell and there we stayed the night and had a sing-song in the canteen tent.

The following morning at 4.00 am the first lift were to leave. We got up with the boys and saw them off in the trucks and then passed the time away poking about amongst the tents, which were full of magazines, grenades and ammunition, that the Parachute boys had been unable to carry.

We listened to the BBC news, anxious to hear if there was any new advance – no! Monty was still 60 miles back. The clouds and mist had not lifted by 8.00 am, when the boys were due to leave. An hour went by, then another hour, all the time we were listening for the sound of the bomber engines warming up and taking off. Then, about 10.30 am on that Sunday morning we stood on that field and watched them. Tug 'planes and gliders were going up into the sky from everywhere, north, south, east and west, all round us. The sky was filling up with 'planes and gliders and then they began circling for height. Round and round they flew, some circling low, others turning south east and making for the big stream of aircraft now flying towards Holland.

Truly a wonderful sight – as I stood on that field that morning, I said to my mate, 'You know, we're seeing history made right now – in years to come, we will read of this in books at home.' Little did we think of the name we were to blaze across the world in that following week, the name of Arnhem.

We stood and watched the sky that morning until every 'plane and glider was a small spot in the distant sky. We didn't say anything, most of us had our own thoughts. I guess most of us had that queer empty feeling inside of our body, that feeling of tension and excitement. So, as I said, we just stood and watched, then slowly walked away to the tents. Two or three of us started scrounging around the now empty tents, picking up a magazine here and there, glancing at a few letters that boys had emptied out of their pockets, picking up an extra hand grenade or two. All the time thinking of the time and picturing where the boys would be.

As the time drew close to 2.00 pm we went into the recreation tent where there was a radio and there we waited for the news that we knew was soon to be given out. There was not much said about the landing – only that Airborne troops had dropped in three different areas of Holland.

We wondered how it was going – was there any fighting, were the boys going on O.K. Later in the day we had a message sent from Division HQ to say that the casualties going over were light, a few down in the sea, a few down over Holland, but the boys were in contact with the enemy. That sounded ever so calm and unimportant – 'contact with the enemy!' Little did we think or know of the terrible fighting and slaughter that was going on in those fields of Arnhem that very afternoon. Little did we think that some of our mates had already died, only 2 hrs after leaving England.

We laid about most of that day, the Officers kept us busy cleaning up the camp and then in the evening we were told to have a sleep as we had to be up about 4.00 am in the morning – 'sleep' they said! – who could sleep? It was our turn in the early morning, we had a thousand things to think about. It took us a long time to drop off to sleep.[1]

1   The 7th KOSB had gliders in the first lift, 56 Horsas and 1 Hamilcar. The Horsas flying in men, jeeps, trailers and the 6 pdr Anti-Tank guns. The one Hamilcar allocated to the Battalion flew in the 2 Bren Gun carriers. The Horsas chalks were as follows:
12 Horsas from RAF Blakehill Farm heading for LZ S taking Battalion HQ, part of HQ Company, A Company and part of Support Company
44 Horsas from RAF Down Ampney heading for LZ S taking B, C and D Companies plus the remainder of HQ and Support Companies
1 Hamilcar from RAF Tarrant Rushton heading for LZ Z
The following arrived safely: all the Horsas from Blakehill Farm, 34 from Down Ampney and the 1 Hamilcar. Of the 10 'lost' Horsas, 7 landed in the UK, 2 in the Channel and 1 in Holland away from its intended LZ. Of the 7 UK lost chalks, 6 went to Holland in the second lift and 1 in the third lift.
The second lift should have consisted of 6 Horsas from RAF Down Ampney, 5 taking men of the MT Platoon and vehicles and 1 taking a Platoon from C Company heading for LZ S. Added to these were 6 of the 7 aborts from the first lift. All of these 12 made it safely to LZ S. This left 1 Horsa from the 7th KOSB to take part in the third lift, it was of course an abort from the first lift. It landed safely on LZ S but all the occupants were taken prisoner within minutes of landing.
As stated before the 1st Airborne Division was going to Arnhem in three separate lifts and the first of these managed to take the 1st Parachute Brigade and around 75% of the 1st Airlanding Brigade. The 1st Parachute Brigade was to seize some high ground to the north of Arnhem and various bridges and buildings in Arnhem. The 1st Airlanding Brigade role in the early hours and days was to protect the Landing and Drop Zones for the second and third lifts.
So on the afternoon of the 17th September between 3:00 pm and 4:00 pm the 7th KOSB started moving westwards away from the landing zones towards Ginkel Heath, to protect it for the drop of the 4th Parachute Brigade which was planned to be around 10.00 the following morning.

Men of the 7th KOSB's No.1 Mortar Platoon unloading handcarts from a Horsa on the
17th September (Copyright: Airborne Museum, Oosterbeek)

31

Monday, 18th September 1944

In the early morning we were up and groping our way to the dining tent for breakfast. 'Breakfast' did I say? We had heard of those wonderful big pre-invasion meals that some of the boys had – but that was not for us – no, Sir! It was the usual piece of bacon plus jam and bread. 'What a meal to die on', we said jokingly but for some of us it was not a joke.

We then pulled on equipment and waited for orders to get into the waiting trucks. We eventually climbed in and away we went to Down Ampney 'drome. By now it was daylight and the time must have been about 7.30 am. As the morning before, there was fog and low cloud but it was now lifting a bit, so that we would probably take off about 10.00 am.

When we reached the 'drome we were given a drink of tea and a couple of cheese or jam sandwiches. Then we were marched over the field to the waiting 'planes and gliders. There they stood on the runway, two rows of black, ugly gliders down the centre and each appropriate tug 'plane on the outside of each glider. The very sight of those black, ugly gliders made me feel sick inside and this morning was no exception. We were being towed by 'Dakotas', which rather suited us, and so as we reached the crates we began looking for our own number chalked on the side of the glider – we found ours, fourth from the front. I was with Bob Bell, we looked all around the glider, gave it a pat on the side and said something like 'Well, see us over O.K. old pal'.

Airborne troops board a Horsa glider
(Copyright: Imperial War Museum CH 7789)

In front of a Dakota fuselage a Horsa is used for training in loading and unloading. A
fully equipped Jeep and 6 pounder anti-tank gun in the foreground
(Airborne Museum 'Hartenstein', Oosterbeek)

We then shook hands with our pilots and had a few cheery words and then
checked over all lashing chains etc. and made sure all split pins were straight and
ready for pulling out. We took off equipment and put on lifebelts and then
watched the 'tug' pilots climbing in and calling 'Good luck' to each other. 'Good
luck' indeed – those RAF guys were coming home again in three or four hours. We
were going down with a one-way ticket —but, the RAF had the glory as usual!
WAAFs were lined along the runway waving to each 'plane as it roared into life.

Our time was very close now. We all climbed aboard, we didn't say much, I
guess Bob had that tight, empty feeling the same as I had. There were no cheers, no
heroics, we just had a final look around, shoved a bullet up the 'spout' of the rifle
and then closed the door. We were sat on two seats at the rear, with the door to the
tail open in case we had to use the hatch quickly in the sea. The Jeep and two trailers were between us and the pilots. That was my greatest fear – if the pilots were
shot, we would not have time to squeeze through to the front. We would go crashing down with the glider to certain and horrible death – that was all that I really
feared. The trailer in front of us was loaded with TNT and guncotton etc. – but I
didn't bother much about that, for as I often said to Bob 'If anything at all hits that
trailer, we won't know a thing, the whole show will go up, us and all!' So, with that
consolation of not suffering, we didn't care so much.

We tightened our safety belts and then listened to the roaring of the engines,
waiting for the signal to go. We heard some engines 'open up' louder and louder,
and then as they moved off down the runway the roar faded off again to a steady
drone. The first one went – the second – the third – and now! We were next! Our
'tug' moved in front of us, moved forward slowly until the rope was tight, and then

Airlanding Troops inside a Horsa glider
(Courtesy Robert Sigmond)

the engines opened out into a terrific roar of noise and wind. Then the glider gave a sudden jerk and we were away.

As I had done before, I sat there and saw the ground outside flash by – airmen, trucks, WAAFs, all flashing by, faster and faster. My heart was going at double pumps, I'm sure. I felt the glider lift, we rocked from side to side alarmingly – I think my heart missed a beat or two. I looked out front and I could see the 'Dakota' still tearing along the runway, striving to get that few extra miles per hour to lift and stay lifted. The end of the runway was coming towards us at a terrific speed and then up the 'tug' went and we were airborne!

I guess everyone, including myself, let out held breaths, pilots and crew alike. I looked at Bob and gave him the 'thumb'. 'We're up' I said – he nodded back. We climbed steadily and circled around waiting for others to get up and then we set off in one direction. I looked out of the window, other 'tugs' and gliders were flying along, front, side and to the rear, in wide open formation. I wasn't feeling too good, the glider was swaying up and down as usual. I loosened off my safety belt a little and put my feet up on the trailer and half-lay down on my seat. I had some hard-boiled sweets on a ledge at the side of me and I started sucking these, but I couldn't stop the sickness coming on. Bob got up and looked out of the window, 'We're over the sea' he said. I didn't like the idea of that – the sickness was getting worse. It finally came up and I once more made good use of a 'Bag, Vomit'!

I felt a little better after that and I had a look out – nothing but sea, one or two feathers of foam where a motor-boat was speeding along. I looked out to the side, I couldn't see any other 'planes. I had a twinge of fear, had we lost the others and would we be a lone target? – but, no! We must have been on the outside lane of that long train of aircraft, for a few minutes later Bob looked out and said 'There's a glider going into the sea!' – I guess the rope had snapped.

I lay back again for a few minutes and the next time I looked out we were over the flooded fields of Holland. I could see small patches of ground sticking out of the sea. I heard a high-pitched roar – I listened. Closer! Closer! I looked at Bob, 'Fighters!' I said. I half-believed they were ours, but there was always that chance that some of them would get through. The high whine came up behind – a dozen thoughts passed through my mind. I imagined bullets tearing through the tail of the glider – I expected to hear the rattle of machine guns. Then the whine passed us and went on forward. Once again I let out my held breath and my heart slowed down a 100 beats a minute or so and settled down again to wait for the next reception – Flak!

We didn't have to wait long – all of a sudden there was a sharp Boom! Boom! Boom! Boom! It sounded like a Bofors to me. I held my breath and waited for a shell to come tearing up through the glider. Once more, Boom! Boom! Boom! Boom! I thought to myself 'What a spot to be in! What a fool I am! Sat up here, without a parachute and with a load of high-explosive right in front of my nose!' I looked at Bob, 'Never again' I shouted, above the roar of the engines. I wouldn't have been surprised had my hair turned all grey there and then.

However, very strangely enough – though I was scared stiff – I kept a grip of myself and I was as calm as if I was sat at home. I just sat there chewing and gave Bob an occasional wink – but inside of me I was tight with tension and nervous strain. It's amazing how calm one can be under such circumstances, and even more

LZ S – The RV point for 7th KOSB, 17th September 1944, photo taken June 2003
(Courtesy Niall Cherry)

General view LZ S taken June 2003
(Courtesy Niall Cherry)

amazing how some men do not show the slightest sign of fear or excitement in dangerous places, such men who don't know the meaning of fear and nerves – men who are not afraid to die – I was!

I sat up straight and tucked my legs underneath my seat – I thought, if anything comes up and hits me, it will be better to get it in the legs than the body. After a few minutes we seemed to pass over the 'Flak' batteries for we were left alone. Some of the boys were not so lucky, as some of the gliders were raked with machine gun fire. I was lucky again, for the only gun that actually fired at my glider just missed the starboard wing by about a foot, so I didn't feel so good in the stomach when I saw those tracer shells fly up past me.

We were now getting close to our LZ (landing zone). We put on equipment and checked rifles once more, then fastened safety belts and waited for the landing. The pilot looked back and shouted 'Get ready, here we go'. With that we cast off the rope, the roar of the engines faded away, only the swishing of the wind now. We nosed down, turned a bit, the wing flaps came down, slowed us up a bit, nose down again. I saw a clearing in front, we were going down towards it, then I saw a great thick belt of trees dead in front, we were flying straight for them! A shocking fear came over me, we were going to crash! I felt the glider lift, lift, straining to keep up – then sink down again. I expected those trees to come crashing through the bottom, but no! I was still lucky, I felt a jolt and a rumbling, it sounded like the wheels, but I couldn't believe it. Then we stopped dead.

I snapped open my belt and jumped up and glanced through the window. I saw the green field outside. I shouted to Bob 'Come on Bob, we're down!' I threw open the door and jumped out and dropped flat, waited and looked round, expecting to hear rifle or machine guns any second, but no! Everything was quiet, except

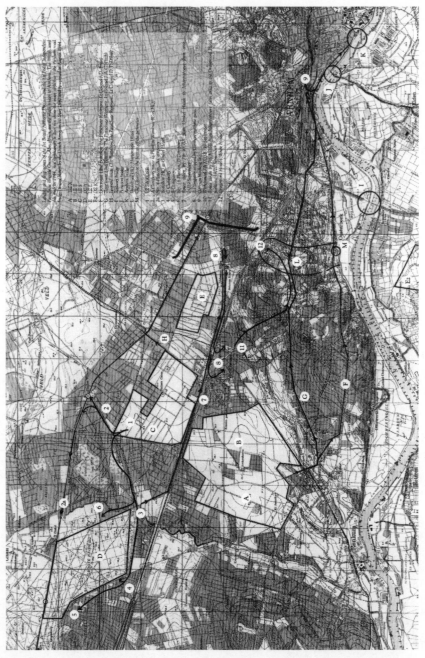

Landing and drop zones of the 1st British Airborne Division and the 1st Polish
Independent Parachute Brigade Group. Also shown are the main routes to Arnhem. The
British used this map in 1944, not surprisingly it does not show the main objective – the
Arnhem road bridge: it was blown by the Dutch Army on 10 May 1940 and re-opened
in August 1944 (Courtesy Robert Sigmond)

(Key to Map on previous page)

A   DZ X
B   LZ Z
C   LZ S
D   DZ Y
E   LZ L
E2   DZ K
F   Lion route (2nd Battalion The Parachute Regiment, Lt Colonel J.D. Frost)
G   Tiger route (3rd Battalion The Parachute Regiment, Lt Colonel J.A.C. Fitch)
H   Leopard route (1st Battalion The Parachute Regiment, Lt Colonel D.T. Dobie)
I   Railway bridge
J   Pontoon bridge
K   Arnhem Bridge
L   Divisional HQ, Hartenstein Hotel
M   Old Church at the bottom of the perimeter

Main movements of the 7th Battalion KOSB:

1   LZ 7th KOSB
2   A Company route to Planken Wambuis (Coy HQ)
2a   No. 4 Platoon, A Company
3   Battalion HQ at Ginkel Heath
4   C Company
5   B Company
6   No. 16 Platoon, D Company
7   Route taken by 7th KOSB from Ginkel Heath to Johannahoeve farm area, 18/
       19 September
8   B Company stopped by German machine guns
9   German blocking line
10   Withdrawal 7th KOSB, 19 September
11   Route taken by 7th KOSB from Johannahoeve farm area to the Dreyeroord
       Hotel position, 19/20 September
12   Dreyeroord Hotel (The White House)

Landing Zone S, 17 September 1944. The sandy track of the unfinished 'Autobahn' (motorway) runs from top left to bottom right. The Rendezvous point was about where the track runs into the woods on the left. Here Piper Willie Ford from Selkirk played 'Blue Bonnets O'er The Border'. The dark lines on the photograph are shadows from the cockpit of the aircraft
(Airborne Museum 'Hartenstein', Oosterbeek)

for the sound of other gliders swishing over us, and the sound of distant guns and mortars. I looked around the field – gliders were laid crashed all over, some still burning, others a tangle of wreckage in the trees – Jeeps, guns and men smashed up together. Then I realised how lucky we had been – some of those poor lads hadn't even got down to the ground, they must have just died where they lay. No-one was able to stop and tend to the wounded for we all had to move and move fast, or be caught by Jerry's fighters as those others had been the day before.

We lay on the ground for a few minutes and watched some of the others coming down, just in case one of them crashed into ours. I still couldn't believe the landing was all over and we were down O.K. What was more, there was no opposition, but we were soon to see the reason for that.

We got back into the glider and while the pilots loosened off the chains, Bob and I cut the wires and released the bolts holding the tail. Now, according to the book, the tail should have dropped off, but these things never behave in action as the drawing office plan, and so the tail still held on. We couldn't tell what was holding it, the bolts were out, the wires cut and before we left Blighty we even cut the fabric round the joint, which was taking a chance on the fabric peeling off. So

At the Landing Zone unloading proceeded at once. An unknown photographer takes two shots of gliders. One of the gliders has 'chalk number' 230 piloted by Staff Sergeant Deakin and Sergeant Butler of the Glider Pilot Regiment. This Horsa flew in six handcarts and the crew of No 1 Mortar Platoon
(Airborne Museum 'Hartenstein', Oosterbeek)

1st positions 7th KOSB:
1 Graaf van Rechterenweg
2 Karel van Gelderlaan
3 Cronjéweg
4 Van Dedemweg
5 Steijnweg
6 Utrechtseweg
7 Oranjeweg
8 Nassaulaan
9 Paul Krugerstraat
10 Bothaweg
11 Hartenweg
12 Stationsweg
= 21st Independent Parachute Company
= Reconnaissance Squadron
= German attacks

there was only one thing to do – crowbars and pick-axes and tear it off! So, with the help of a couple of other lads, we started hacking at the stubborn tail end, for by now we were getting a bit of a sweat on. Any second I was expecting to see Germans coming through the woods and I pictured machine guns ripping through the glider – and us.

We finally prised off the tail and then we started on the unloading. The trailer and Jeep had to be lifted bodily to pull out the steel troughs. These troughs were then fixed to the rear of the body and the first trailer run down – then the Jeep – and then the other trailer. We hooked up and loaded the Jeep with some of the glider equipment and then we were all set to go.

The pilot was a good chap, he gave us a few fags each and took our names and addresses and promised to write to our people if he got back before us. Then off we went, to join up with the rest of the boys. The two pilots came with us until they could form up with their own Regiment. We ran onto a rough track and met another Jeep, Alec Grant and then Bill Milligan. We were pleased to see they had got down O.K. Then all along the side of the track there was slit trenches, foxholes, some had parachutes inside for warmth and dryness. The boys looked round at us, black, dirty faces, some with a fag sticking from the corner of their mouths. We also saw the other boys laid under the trees, some covered over with a parachute – a parachute they would never use again. Also, other boys laid near them, some with faces bandaged, others with legs torn and bloody. It was as I looked at these boys I fully realised we were really in the fighting now, this was no exercise. As I passed these boys in foxholes I also realised why we had been able to land and unload without a fight. These boys had fought and died, but held that ground for us. I had a feeling of being guilty of causing this trouble for them, but I guess they were pleased to see us.

We passed on along the road to the railway crossing called Wolfheze, where we turned left and followed the road alongside the embankment. We passed a few houses on the road, the Dutch peasants were stood at the gates, shaking our hands, begging the parachutes off us. We rested a while. The two pilots left us there to join their own men. We shook hands and thanked them for a good landing, then they moved off. I learned when I got home again that the pilot had died there – like many others, he had a leg blown off and hadn't the medical attention and subsequently died.

Not that we underrate the Medical Corps, no! They did a wonderful job, but like everybody else they had no hospital, or no satisfactory place to perform their duties. Then, after a few days, most of the doctors were captured with the wounded they refused to leave and so the wounded just had to lay somewhere and put on their own field dressings. Of course, the seriously wounded mostly died from loss of blood and lack of attention.

I watched a few Military Police making a couple of German prisoners dig a slit trench. The Jerries sat down and refused to dig – they thought they were digging their own graves. They thought we were desperate men, like their own Parachutists. One of the MPs suddenly hit the Jerry ... that changed his mind – he dug!

We saw a few of our mates and we asked them how things were going. They told us the fighting had been tough the day before. We had lost a whole Company in a desperate bayonet charge. Peter MacFarlane, the COs driver, had been killed.

Ginkel Heath
1 Planken Wambuis
2 Ginkel Pub
3 Huts
4 Ede Barracks
5 Motorway under construction
6 Reijerscamp farm
= German advance
(Crown copyright courtesy Robert Sigmond)

Poor Peter always said he would come back O.K. He was a good lad.[1] Also they had found eight of the Parachute boys all shot together – Jerry was taking no prisoners! I thought, well, either we pull through now or not at all. Of course, we couldn't take many prisoners, so I guess we couldn't expect much from Jerry.

We moved up past the woods – parachutes and containers were hanging from the trees in hundreds. Whenever I got the chance I dashed to a container and opened it to try to find either a machine gun or food. I couldn't find either, every one that I opened had bombs or shells in it.

We now split up a bit, our four ammunition Jeeps and trailers were driven into a path at the side of the road and there we had to stop until we got orders. It was now very dark so that every figure moving about was treated with suspicion. If

1   3194351 L/Cpl P MacFarlane's date of death according to the Commonwealth War Graves Commission is 18th September 1944 and was first buried by the side of a stream in a wood to the north of the Amsterdamseweg. This road goes towards Ginkel Heath from the area north of LZ S. He was aged 28 and is now in the Arnhem/Oosterbeek CWGC cemetery plot 23 row A grave 2.

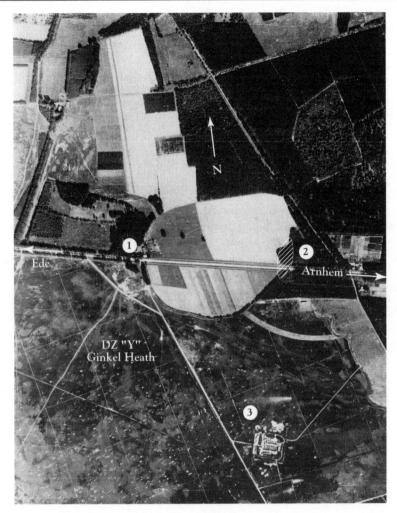

Ginkel Heath
1 Ginkel Pub
2 Positions of No 4 Platoon A Company, held until early morning 18 September
3 The huts on Ginkel Heath. The positions of No 16 Platoon D Company
(Crown Copyright, courtesy of Robert Sigmond)

someone came along we would stare and wait until he was close up to us, keeping our rifles and bayonets on him and then whisper 'Who is it?'

We settled down by the Jeeps, I propped my back against a tree and watched and listened for any movement in the woods. We couldn't sleep, we had to be on the alert all the time. Every little noise in the woods made us start and grip our rifles tight. The boys were having a tough fight in the woods a little way in front – a machine gun nest was holding them up. Stray bullets slashed through the trees, we kept down low.[2]

Ginkel Heath, 18 September. Moments before the drop of 4th Parachute Brigade. A single glider can be seen. It would also land on the zones near Wolfheze. None ever landed on Ginkel Heath. The heather is burning as the result of mortar fire. The motorway under construction can be seen at the bottom of the photograph and the Ginkel Pub and Ede-Arnhem road are at the top.
(Airborne Museum 'Hartenstein', Oosterbeek)

2   After protecting DY Y on the 17th and 18th of September the 7th KOSB were on the move again to the area of LZ L about 3 miles away. This was another large open space on which the third lift was to land. The third lift mainly consisted of gliders carrying men and equipment from the 1st Polish Parachute Brigade.

32

Tuesday, 19th September 1944

All that long night we sat there listening, watching and fighting to keep awake, then towards dawn we moved up the road to where the boys were dug in. We had to cross over a wide, open field to a big, white house (the Johannahoeve farm) over the other side. This ground was where the next reinforcements were going to land, so that we had to hold it at all costs. We did – for about 24 hours.

2nd positions 7th KOSB (Courtesy of Robert Sigmond)
1 Graaf van Rechterenweg, 2 Karel van Gelderlaan, 3 Cronjéweg,
4 Van Dedemweg, 5 Steijnweg, 6 Utrechtseweg, 7 Oranjeweg
8 Nassaulaan, 9 Paul Krugerstraat, 10 Bothaweg, 11 Hartenweg
12 Stationsweg = Glider Pilots

Johannahoeve farm seen in a southerly direction. B Company advanced from the right-hand side passing the main house and farm buildings as far as the buildings on the left-hand side. Here German machine-gun fire stopped the advance and Major Forman withdrew to the main farm and took up a position along the tree-lined lane in the foreground.
(Courtesy Robert Sigmond)

We got across to the house O.K., there was a big, square yard at the rear of the house, surrounded by hay-barns, etc. At first we drove the Jeeps and trailers into a big barn until we realised that if this place was hit, we would loose the whole lot. So we dispersed the Jeeps in the yard, which now was not too healthy, for an occasional bullet would whine over and knock a piece of plaster off the house. Whether these were stray shots or whether it was a sniper I don't know, but anyway, we kept down behind the low wall and crossed the yard at the double.

Bob and I managed to get a 'brew' going, crouched down behind an old cart. The 'brew' was half on the boil when Jerries mortaring came pretty close, but mortars or not I was determined to have that 'char'. So I crouched down low behind an old plough and coaxed on the 'brew'. We finally did get a drink of 'char' and felt a bit better. I was feeling pretty tired for we had no sleep during the night and there was no prospect of any during the day, so I just had to keep moving around and keep my eyes open. This wasn't hard during the day because there was so much going on – mortaring, sniping and we were constantly on the lookout for Germans, but at night it was terribly hard to keep awake.

The Jeeps were wanted for bringing in the wounded. The First Aid Post we had about 300 yards away had been taken by the enemy, together with Doctors and Orderlies.[1] So we had to form a Post in a small cottage nearby the farm, our own

1   It would appear that Albert was misinformed about the medical personnel as the 7th's RMO (Regimental Medical Officer) Captain B Devlin RAMC wasn't taken prisoner until the 21st of September.

Johannahoeve Farm, as seen today, home to some of the 7th KOSB's during their defence of LZ-L (Copyright: Martin Middlebrook)

Padre and stretcher bearers doing what they could. Strangely enough, the Germans allowed Jeeps to drive into their lines to our captured First Aid Post. Of course, we were taking prisoners right to them, so I suppose they looked at it that way, rather than wanting to tend to our wounded.

We then moved outside the farm onto the track leading around the Landing Zone around the farmhouse. We had to dig in there and be prepared to hold off any German attack until the 'lift' came in that morning. About 10.00 am the RSM came along and said we were to go out for ammunition and supplies, to collect from the parachute containers dotted all over the ground and in the trees.

We set off with empty trailers and began opening containers and collecting mortar bombs and machine guns. It was warm work tussling with the containers with all our equipment on, but we didn't dare take it off for one minute. We collected quite a few bombs and then we heard 'planes coming – the next lift was due in at 10.30 am. We thought this must be the fighter escort. We looked up through the trees, I counted nine fighters. I looked at them but I couldn't see the markings on them. The engines sounded like Germans to me – the 'planes looked like 'Thunderbolts'.

The next second, the leader turned and dived straight for us. We didn't wait any longer. Bob Bell, Teddy Woodcock and I dived into a shallow sandpit about one foot deep. The first fighter tore across the trees, cannon and machine guns rattling. I dug my face into the sand, the cannon shells burst over the ground, right across us. I lay and waited tense, for the bullets to tear into my back – they missed! The next one came over, cannons barking, exploding across the ground in a stream. I hugged the ground, I thought 'This is the end – they're sure to get us', but, no!

A British soldier unpacking a radio container
(Copyright: Imperial War Museum BU1113)

They all missed us. After each one I said 'Are you O.K., Bob, Ted?' 'Yes, are you?' came the replies. 'I wish I was back in Boston!' I replied.

I raised my head and looked across the ground to where there was a small tunnel under the track through the wood. This tunnel had been for a small stream presumably, but now it was dry. With or without water, it looked like heaven to me. I said 'As soon as this next one passes, Bob, dive out and follow me'. That was what they did – follow me – for I covered that 20 yards in about 2 seconds flat! There were four or five other lads in there too. We had a little laugh at each other when we tore in. 'Someone chasing you?' one enquired. That was the typical humour and spirit of the boys at the front – a thing the Germans just could not understand.

I had a look at my rifle, it was choked with sand and dirt. I got out my pull-through and a bit of rag and cleaned it up best I could. At least I made sure it worked, I never knew when I was going to need it – fast! The fighters passed over, having set fire to a farmhouse near to us, where, incidentally, we had a big store of ammunition. I wondered if they had been told, I didn't know whether to trust some of the Dutch, but what else could they say with a gun in their ribs, probably.

We got our Jeeps back onto the road, constantly watching the trees and hedges for Germans. That was how it was all the time – someone would shout 'Look out! There's some Jerries in the woods there!'. We would then stop, crouching down, finger on trigger, watching for the slightest movement amongst the high grass. If only the Jerries came out and showed themselves, we could at least have it out with them and shoot it out, but no! They kept well under cover, sniping, whenever we moved. I guess they were not strong enough, so they thought, or else they were scared stiff of us 'Red Devils'.

I think the reason why they didn't mass attack and wipe us out was because they thought we were strong in number and I don't think the Germans were ever inclined to make an attack if they didn't know how strongly they were outnumbered. As it happened, it was us who were sadly outnumbered, for around the farm we were only a handful. Most of the lads had gone up into the woods where Jerry was well dug in and holding the way into Arnhem.

The Germans in that area had the job of stopping us getting to the Parachute Battalions in Arnhem and they did that job – they did stop us. Every move we made, they stopped us with men, machine guns, mortars, tanks, flame-throwers, fighters and everything else they could find. They threw everything they had at us. I remember saying to my pal, 'It wouldn't surprise me to see old pans and kettles coming over next!'

We spread out the Jeeps along the lane and then started digging a couple of foxholes for ourselves. Alec Grant and I stayed along by the white farmhouse and

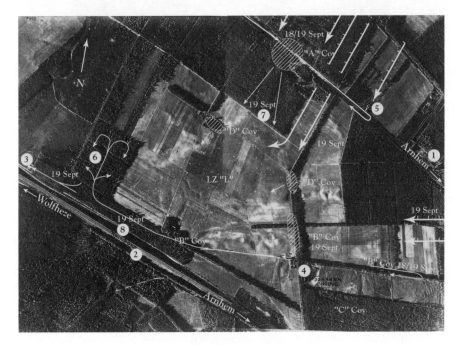

1 Amsterdamseweg
2 Railway Ede-Arnhem, between Wolfheze and Oosterbeek on a high embankment
3 Direction Wolfheze close to the culvert
4 Johannahoeve farm, Battalion Headquarters
5 Schweizer Höhe
6 B Company's 'Polish Glider wood'
7 Edge of wood were part of A Company ran into the Germans
8 Brigadier Hackett, 4th Parachute Brigade Headquarters
= German attacks
Burnt out gliders and parachutes of the supply drop are clearly visible on LZ L
(Courtesy of Robert Sigmond)

A formation of RAF Stirlings drop supplies on Tuesday 19th as flak explodes around
them (Copyright: IWM BU1092)

dug in under the trees and bushes – then we waited for the welcome reinforcements
that we expected.

All that time those German machine guns in the woods never stopped once.
One particularly heavy .45 machine gun chattered all that day. Some of the boys
came down to the farm from time to time for water. They were dishevelled and
clothing torn with the bushes, faces black and haggard, some with a head or arm
bandaged. Those boys up there were having a tough time and I guess the casualties
must have been pretty heavy, for the mortars were pouring down all the time.

Eventually, the hay-barn behind us caught fire, which didn't improve our foxhole any. We were showered with embers and smoke, but we stuck it out. In the
field opposite were two horses, they galloped from one end to the other, crazy with
the bursting bombs and firing – I felt sorry for them. Then the old folk came out of
the farmhouse, young, old and kids, they looked at us and made wild signs with
their arms – which way should they go? We pointed across the field away from the
wood. The old women had a bundle of blankets and a few belongings, I guess, on
their backs. I watched them stumbling away as best they could, helping along a
poor, old Grannie. It sort of touched me to see such things. I felt that it was us that
had brought this trouble to them, but such is War. If only we could fight without
bringing such trouble and suffering to old, innocent people.

We heard the drone of 'planes coming – we listened, they got louder and
louder. All those 'planes were sure to be ours … and then we saw them, coming
across the countryside low. Stirlings, Dakotas, gliders, hundreds of them – what a

sight! Such a great defying roar of engines, as if saying 'Nothing can stop us' and then as we watched it seemed like at a given signal every German Ack-Ack and machine gun opened up together. Tracer shells and bullets tore up and into those bombers and gliders. I watched and my heart dropped into my boots. Stirlings were on fire, Dakotas were on fire, but still they flew on, dropping supplies, the sky was full of coloured parachutes, drifting down, down to Jerry. If only we could tell them, those good lads were flying through Hell and dying with their 'planes to drop supplies that we couldn't possibly get. A Stirling past over us, engine blazing but still the boys were pushing out the containers. I watched until it crashed.

Then the gliders cut loose, half a dozen made for the field opposite, the first two came in low, heading straight for Jerry, saw their mistake and endeavoured to turn and drop the other way. They lost flying speed, stalled and hit the ground heavily. We saw some of the boys run from the wreckage, but only a few ran out, the rest were probably shot to pieces up there – what a Hell of a way to die! I watched another glider hover slowly over the field, I could see tracer bullets pouring into it, the nose dropped steeply. I thought for a second he was dodging the Flak, and then he tilted right onto his nose and came straight down, straight into the ground. I dropped my eyes for a second, I couldn't watch it hit the ground – perhaps it was full of lads, I don't know, it was horrible to see. It's one thing seeing lads go down fighting, but another thing to see them go down without a chance. I looked at Alec and said 'If ever I get out of this, I'll never take a chance like that again – never!' It was then I realised what a chance I had taken the day before and how lucky I had been to get through.

Amongst the hundreds of containers floating down came four or five Paratroopers of the Polish Brigade. All of them were supposed to drop, but as the Flak was so heavy they didn't drop, apart from the few we saw[2]. These men dropped in the field opposite us, one of them hung in the inevitable tree but he managed to get loose and drop down. The others dashed here and there for a minute, they hardly knew which way to run and then they saw some of our boys and made towards them. We then got a shout that Jerries were coming through the wood. I dashed up towards Bob Bell's Jeep just in case we were moving. I told them I thought Jerries were coming through the wood. There were only five of us together, one had a Bren-gun. I grabbed the Vickers machine gun that we had on the Jeep, then we crouched down and watched the trees, finger on trigger, tense, thoughts running through my mind. 'Suppose a lot came and we couldn't stop them?' 'What if we got to grips with bayonets?' 'What would it feel like to be bayoneted?' 'Maybe I'll die here!' 'How would Mum take it back home?' All these thoughts run through a man's head in the few seconds he waits to fight to a death[3].

2   There is a possibility Albert was incorrect here as, to the best of my knowledge, the first paratroopers from the Polish Brigade landed south of the Rhine on 21st September.

3   The third lift consisted of 44 gliders, 35 originally planned to go on this day plus 9 chalks which had aborted on earlier lifts over the UK. The 'retries' were instructed to land on their original LZ but some pilots chose to ignore this instruction and landed on LZ L. 15 Horsas flying from RAF Keevil carried the glider element of the 1st Polish Parachute Brigade. The loads consisted of HQ, Signals, Medical and Transport and Supply Company men and equipment. 20 Horsas took off from RAF Tarrant Rushton carrying 20 jeeps, 10 trailers, 10 6 pdr Anti-Tank guns, 16 motorcycles and 74 men

One of the gliders carrying Polish equipment shortly before landing on Landing Zone L,
the fields of Johannahoeve farm
(Copyright: Captain H.B. Booty, in 1944 Staff Captain 4th Parachute Brigade)

Just then Capt. Clayhills, our Adjutant, ran up and said, 'Get these Jeeps away,
quickly – down the road, anywhere!' We didn't need to be told twice. We piled in,
tore into the wire fence, broke through, across the field and onto the road again
over the other side.

Further down the road we came up to the Polish 6 pounder Anti-tank guns
and trucks. We squeezed past them and down the road alongside the railway

Polish airborne troops. There was much confused fighting in the area around LZ L on
the 19th, particularly in the woods to the north and east where the 10th and 156th
Parachute Battalions were trying to punch a hole through to Arnhem. These attacks
failed and in the early afternoon the commander of the 4th Parachute Brigade
(Brigadier J Hackett) ordered both units to disengage and withdraw in the direction in
Wolfheze. It just so happened that whilst they were doing this the gliders carrying the
poles came into land. With the Germans hot on the heels of the 4th Brigade men the
gliders appeared as easy targets. It is believed that only 3 of the 6 pdr guns were able to be
removed from their Horsas. Meanwhile after doing their best to protect LZ L the 7th
KOSB (or those still with the Battalion as quite a number had been taken prisoner on
this day in the woods), skilfully led by the CO Colonel Payton Reid managed to get into
the village of Oosterbeek about 2 miles south of LZ L. The 4th Parachute Brigade for
reasons best known to its commander decided to spend the night in the area of
Wolfheze and only made it to Oosterbeek on the 20th with only a fraction of the
number who had dropped on DY Y two days before. The 7th KOSB were allocated a
section in the north of Oosterbeek to defend, as all ideas to reach Arnhem had now been
forgotten. It was hoped that if an area north of the Rhine could be held XXX Corps
could still attempt a river crossing. The perimeter in Oosterbeek was basically a
horseshoe shape with the base of the shoe being on the river.

embankment. This was a high embankment, we drew into the gorse and trees alongside and asked what was happening. It seemed like the Jerries were closing in all round, attacking, and we were running! We were not strong enough or organised to hold off a big attack, as was the trouble from the beginning, we were split up too much. I looked along the embankment. I thought if they plaster this hollow now, we've all had it.

We moved along again and up to a low tunnel that passed under the railway – this tunnel was only just high enough to allow a Jeep to get through, then someone got jammed inside. I said 'Come on, Bob, let's go up to the level crossing' about ¼ mile along at Wolfheze. I jumped in and Bob put his foot down. The machine gun firing was very close and we tore up that track. I looked round at the second trailer and I thought of that TNT and gelignite bouncing up and down. There was a big cloud of dust behind us, which was good for us. Whether or not they were firing at us I didn't know, I just crouched low in the seat and hoped for the best.

We passed over the crossing and onto the road and turned left to find everyone else was like us. Nobody knew which way to go. We followed another Jeep down the road, he turned up a road to the right – wrong way!

We managed to turn again, back onto the road again and back the way we came. We went up as far as the crossing again and then an Officer shouted 'Down the road to HQ towards Oosterbeek', on the outskirts of Arnhem.

We followed the rest of the mixture of Jeeps, etc. going down the road, past a row of bungalows. The people were standing at the doors waving to us and giving the 'V' sign. We stopped every few yards to let some lads who were walking climb on, and picked up others who were wounded. We had twelve on at the finish, mostly lads wounded and bloody. One lad had no gun, he asked if we had a spare

The tunnel under the railway through which the 4th Para Brigade passed
(Copyright: Glenn Schoen)

and I said he could have the Vickers machine gun if he could use it – he took it. As we drove down the road a Newsreel cameraman was stood on the roadside following us with his camera – just as if he was back home somewhere.

We reached a big green and a HQ had been formed there in a large house. We started digging slit trenches or foxholes amongst the bushes. No sooner had we got a hole dug when someone started sorting us out – Border Regiment here – Staffs here – KOSBs there – we moved off again into some wood behind the house. There we started digging again, it was terribly hard digging, the ground was full of roots and stony. It was getting dark and I had to dig by feeling the ground. I eased off a bit and then I heard a 'Moaning Minnie' for the first time, a multiple mortar that sent over eight bombs together giving a terrible dying moan. I picked up the shovel and dug – and dug fast!

We were only there an hour or so and then moved again, getting all mixed up with other Jeeps and guns. We pulled along the road a little way and drew into the side. We lined the Jeeps along a wall, about four Jeeps and trailers, then we sat down a bit and waited. Nothing happened – it was pitch dark, everything was strangely quiet – four of us dropped into a slit trench Jerry had made and we slept for a couple of hours.

33

Wednesday, 20th September 1944

When dawn came, one of the boys said Jerry had been snooping around the houses across the road. It was a good job for us that the Jeeps were in the dark against the wall.

A Jeep came along when it was daylight, we had to follow him. We went along past the HQ again and headed into the suburbs. We drove along watching every house, every corner. We turned right and then right again into the grounds of a big Hotel, 'The White House' we called it[1]. We dispersed the Jeeps around the garden and started digging once more. Bill Milligan came along with me and we got a good-sized slit trench dug. All the other lads were doing the same, for once Jerry got our position we knew we would be 'dead-ducks' if we weren't below ground level.[2]

We were not left in peace long – snipers began closing in through the trees. Those hellish snipers, we couldn't see them and we couldn't keep our heads up to look for them. The firing drew in closer – they seemed to be coming in from three sides. Arthur Green came along asking for hand grenades – he got a box out of a trailer and the three of us crouched around 'priming' them with detonators.

Then we heard a clattering of tracks coming down the road, lucky for us it was a half-track. Someone shouted for a PIAT (Projector Infantry Anti-Tank) – they must have got one, for as the half-track came in front of us, a loud explosion envel-

1 This was the Hotel Dreyeroord situated on the Graaf van Rechterenweg by the station in north Oosterbeek.

2 When arriving in the Divisional area in Oosterbeek the Battalion received orders confirming that they were to hold the northern part of the perimeter covering the railway. There were already parties of Glider pilots, Engineers and men from the 21st Independent Parachute Company in this area and the Battalion was to extend the line held by them to the east. The CO chose his position from his map, he selected a small wood close to the houses almost immediately to the east of the 21st Company's positions. Colonel Payton Reid and Major Coke set out to contact the 21st men and recce the chosen position. Eventually the position selected was the grounds and gardens of two large houses. This is what Payton Reid later wrote: 'I do not think that any who were there will forget the White House and its surroundings. When I knocked at its door about 9pm on 19th September all was peace and quiet. Had I dropped from Mars I could scarcely have aroused more interest and I was immediately greeted as a liberator by the numerous occupants, - it was, I found, a small hotel. Never have I felt such a hypocrite. I had come to announce my intention of placing soldiers in the grounds and vicinity and the delight with which this news was received was most touching- but at the same time most pathetic, as I knew I was bringing them only danger and destruction. By the next night the building was reduced to a shell and its inmates were crouching uncomfortably in the cellar.'

In the early days at Oosterbeek the Battalion was located as follows:
C Company (which was the strongest numerically) around the Karel van Gelderlaan
D Company around the Graaf van Rechterenweg and the van Dedemweg
B Company holding the southern part of the Cronjeweg

Hotel Dreyeroord
(Courtesy Robert Sigmond)

oped it – it stopped. The top opened, everybody blazed away at the top – I fired as fast as I could pull trigger at the dim figures in the smoke. Someone shouted 'Cease fire!' If those Jerries weren't shot, they fried inside for it burnt all day.

Bill was crouched in the bottom of the trench, I nudged him and said 'It's O.K. Bill, get up'. It was then I thought he was going to pieces, he wasn't a coward, like many others he just didn't have the nerve. I was just as scared myself many times, but my strong will just kept me from letting myself go to pieces. Bill was one of the best, but he was a very meek, small fellow and old compared to us – he should never have been in a spot like that.

Snipers were in some good positions amongst the woods and houses in the distance, and were taking a steady toll of the boys who were a bit careless in keeping down. We were lucky to have a brick wall just behind us and on our left, amongst the trees, were our boys and so we only had to watch our right and front.

Somebody over by the house was calling for stretcher-bearers. I heard our Second-in-Command, Major Coke, come over and ask what was wrong. He looked across the garden and then started walking over. If it had been one of the boys we would have told him to get himself down, but Major Coke was Major Coke, so we just watched. He only walked about six paces, then, Bang! Bang! Two quick shots - –he dropped! One of the boys helped him back to a slit trench – he was a bit shocked. I could hear him talking, he asked how far was the RAP (Regimental Aid Post)? Was it possible to dig a communication trench to the RAP? 'I wonder what the men will think of me?' he said.

Major J Coke's grave 2004. Died 18th November 1944 aged 33, buried in Arnhem Oosterbeek War Cemetery – 23.B.17 'Faithful unto death' (Editor's collection)

Bill was down in the trench, I told him Johnny Coke had just been hit – I didn't like to tell him. Over on my right I was watching a lad looking over his foxhole. I saw the ground spurt up in front of him, his face fell onto the earth. That was how it was – those snipers just wore us down. The mortaring was getting close, plastering our positions, two bearers went past with Teddy Woodcock on the stretcher. He gave us a little salute as he went past, as if he was 'riding-in-State'.

The CO came up, he was expecting an attack. He told us to spread the Jeeps out a bit. One of the trailers was on fire, ammunition exploding in all directions. The boys took most of the Jeeps down the wood. Mortars were dropping all around us. We were told to spread out a bit and be ready for them. I doubled across the wood a little way and dropped behind a big tree. I hadn't much cover – I thought I heard a bullet or two 'zip' near me – this was no place for me!

I jumped up again, ran back towards an empty foxhole – I fell in just as a shot sounded – the boys thought they'd got me. I was only there a few minutes, then the barn nearby caught fire, horses and cattle were in there. The noise was awful, some of the boys tried to stop the fire – no use! I dashed over near to a small cottage that was the RAP, it was full of wounded – I dropped into a deep slit trench outside.

There was a heavy drone of aircraft coming – I watched the sky. There they were – Stirlings, Dakotas, parachutes dropping by the hundred, most of them dropping to Jerry. Those that fell anywhere near us were no use, for Jerry had snipers covering the ground. The Flak was taking a heavy toll of our supply 'planes – Jerry had brought up Flak guns all along the route, for he knew where they were heading and so he was ready for them. I watched for Paratroops to drop, but none came. 'If only they would send us more men', I thought. I watched them head back for home and the drone faded once more in the distance.

I got up again and ran across to some slit trenches near the road. Sgt. Danny Keyes was there with some of his boys. They had a 6 pounder anti-tank gun pointing down the road. Then snipers got the gun covered, so that they had to lay a few yards away and fire it by a long cord when a tank showed down the road. It didn't do much good, but the thought of it kept Jerry at bay. A half-track came rattling down the road – a shout for a PIAT – a couple of bombs went – the half-track stopped – the crew managed to get away.

It was now getting dark, we were told to stand by for an attack. However, Jerry didn't try, he must have thought we were strong. I lay down the best I could, every time someone passed over the trench a shower of dirt and earth came down on me – more than once someone fell in on top of me. I was hungry and tired, I hadn't had a meal since I landed!

Withdrawal of 4th Parachute Brigade and the 7th Battalion and the formation of the Perimeter
1 Divisional Headquarters, Hartenstein Hotel
2 White House
(Crown Copyright, courtesy Robert Sigmond)

34

Thursday, 21st September 1944

A scared voice up the road shouted 'Look out boys, Jerry's using gas!' Whether Jerry was up to his tricks of making hissing noises or whether it was a Jerry shouting, I don't know. It certainly put the fear of Hell into me. I thought of choking with gas – 'I've had it now!' – nothing came. Just after that someone called 'Halt!' in the garden behind – no reply. Then a couple of shots in the dark – that was that.

At last the dawn came – 'How long was this going on? – What was news this morning? – Where was the Second Army? – What would today bring?' I thought I'd get back to HQ Company, the mortaring was terrific, all the time bullets were exploding above us, making a terrific crackling, breaking our nerve. Our mortars were just behind me, they deafened me when they fired. I heard the Officer ask how many rounds we had left. 'Seven each mortar' came back the reply – I thought we had just about 'had it'.

The mortars were dropping all around us, every time one dropped someone would cry out for stretcher-bearers. I thought 'Anytime now one will get me, I couldn't last forever without being hit or killed'. I jumped out and ran back to the garden and saw a few of the MT boys in foxholes. I lay down near a tree – mortar bombs dropped all around and I hugged the ground.

Then I ran across to a slit trench. I was only there a few minutes when Jerry brought up a loudspeaker van, bands played. I thought the whole German Army was coming! A voice spoke in English and gave quite a speech. 'Gentlemen of the 1st Airborne Division' it started, 'You are surrounded, your Second Army cannot reach you, surrender now! Remember your women, your wives and families – why fight on?' On and on it went, trying to break our spirit. Somebody sent over a PIAT bomb, some of the boys shouted 'Come and get us!' What spirit! Boys like that couldn't be beaten – boys did I say? We were all men now, men weary with battle, seeing death, boys turned into men overnight.

The CO gave the alarm 'Here they come!' 'Take positions!' I dived into a slit trench and watched the hedges and houses across the field. Behind me and on the left some of the Officers were getting the boys together for an attack. Jerry came down the woods, shouting and howling. I heard the boys were falling back. All sorts of thoughts ran through my mind 'This was the end – I would die fighting with a bayonet'. A mortar bomb exploded a few yards away with a loud bang and a flash – somehow the splinters missed me. I watched the far hedge, I thought I saw something move, I fired a few shots – no more movement! The noise was terrific, Sten guns barking, boys shouting. I heard our lads start shouting 'Charge!' – they were fighting back.

Ten or fifteen minutes later it was quiet again. The boys had stopped them. The cottage behind was now on fire – the wounded! – My God! – the wounded! We got orders to clear out. I drew back into a corner of the garden, there were only about four of us there. The CO told us to get the wounded away. Mortar bombs were still dropping, two of the wounded lads on the stretchers asked us to get them

121

Sgt. Graham's grave 2004. Died 21st September 1944 aged 32, buried in Arnhem Oosterbeek War Cemetery – 17.A.8 'Lovingly remembered by his wife and two little girls, Hilary and Jillian' (Editor's collection)

away. We tried to comfort them and they cried for us to get them away from the bombs. Someone brought up a half-wrecked Jeep and we managed to lift them on. Some Dutch civvies came up with two more wounded – God bless them! They shook hands with us and passed on.

The CO told us to get the men round to the RAP in a big house. I expected to see the boys coming back from the woods, but not many came back. Our casualties had been very heavy in the wood near the White House. Our Provost Sgt., Sgt. Graham, had died leading the boys in that charge, so had Major Cochran (OC HQ Company) and many of the other boys. Capt. Clayhills (Adjutant) later said he had time to bury some of them in the slit trenches – slit trenches that we had dug ourselves, that those boys had dug –

only to be laid in them, dead. Many had dug their own graves in the wood that day – many did not come back.

We got the rest of the wounded onto the Jeep and the four of us walked alongside holding the stretchers on. As we turned the corner of the road up to the RAP I quite expected to be shot down by some sniper. We had laid our rifles in the Jeep, just in case, and probably that saved our lives, for I'm pretty sure some of those snipers must have had a 'bead' on us, but seeing we were unarmed and with wounded, let us go. We passed one or two of our boys laid along the road, they were laying just as they had fallen – face down, helmets still fastened under their chins.

We went up the drive to the large house taken over by our Medical Corp

Major Cochran's grave 2004. Died 20th September 1944 aged 31, buried in Arnhem Oosterbeek War Cemetery – 20.C.7 'Always remembered with great love and pride' (Editor's collection)

The battle damaged house of Kate Ter Horst, as seen in 1945 from a photograph taken by C. van Rijn (Copyright: Renkum Municipal Archives)

and we handed the wounded over to an Orderly. I was parched, so I asked for a mouthful of water. 'Sorry, there's none to spare, we want it for the wounded' came the reply. There was no more to be said, that was good enough for me, when I glanced around at those poor lads I turned and walked out – dry!

Out in the garden we had half a dozen Jeeps left, all our own had been lost at the White House, together with my pack and rations. There were four of our boys there and a Signal chap near a Jeep. I squatted down beside him and had a few words with him. He shared a bar of chocolate with me. I looked around for a place to dig a foxhole, most of the other lads had dug slit trenches for themselves. It was now quite dark, I wandered round by the bushes in the garden. I saw some heaps amongst the grass and along the bushes so I bent down and had a closer look. Then I realised they were our dead lads laid there – just laying in the grass, close together! I turned and walked back, feeling a bit sick in the stomach.

I got out my entrenching tool (small spade) and started on a hole big enough for myself. I felt the ground and dug a few inches out, about 2½ ft. wide and 6 ft. long. I was kneeling down and I stopped for a spell, I was dead-beat. I pulled myself together, – 'I must keep on digging' – I dug a few more inches out, feeling the ground with one hand, shoving the spade in with the other. I lay down to see what it was like for length and closed by eyes. I could have dropped to sleep in a second, I shook myself – 'I must dig a trench first' – I dug a bit more out. I was feeling sick to death, it was now pitch dark, I couldn't see any of the other boys and I felt alone and miserable in the dark.

All this time the rattle of a Sten gun would sound from time to time. Some of the boys were a bit 'itchy on the trigger' in the dark. We were there for an hour or so longer and then an Officer came along and said we were to get the Jeeps and the Bren Gun Carrier ready to move. We were to try and join the rest of the unit. There was a quiet "conflab" with some of the boys who said they knew the way to our Div. HQ.

We moved out as quiet as possible, on the road we joined up with more Jeeps and away we went at walking speed. Some of the boys walked warily in front. We either walked near the front or sat on the front wing of the Jeeps. We had to do this because it was so dark the drivers couldn't see the Jeep in front. I sat on the front wing of one Jeep, rifle at the ready, finger on trigger – any second we might run into some Jerries.

On we went, down the road and finished up round a green of some sort – we stopped! I thought to myself, 'What a spot to be in – in a strange town – Jerries all around us – pitch dark …. and us lost!' I said to the driver 'This is what I often said would happen back home, lost in the enemy territory – and now here we are!' The Officer had another 'conflab' and off we moved again.

We got onto a narrow lane, came to a drive down to a big house and in the gate we went. As we reached the house a dark figure past by me only 6 ft. away. He past over the lawn and then turned and fired two shots with a revolver. We were all startled and jumped away quickly, my driver and I crouched behind the corner of the house. It was not the single figure we were getting out the way of, but maybe there were more of them in the darkness.

We then found out we were in the wrong place, so the trailers had to be hooked off to turn the Jeeps round. We managed this and then started off again down the road. Our boys were walking down the lane in single file, we nosed past them, hitting the wall occasionally, got tangled up in wire, had a few awkward minutes getting free again and then on again.

We finally came to a small group of cottages, a lot of the boys were sat around in the dark. I heard Bob Bell's voice in the dark, Henry Steele was sat with him. I sat down and got the 'gen' from him. He had lost his Jeep, he asked what had happened to me and I told him my story. Meanwhile the CO was moving around and getting us all together. He took us down the road a short way and told us to split up between the houses and dig in. He was making one of the cottages his HQ and we were to form a defence all round. This was to be our final stand, no more moves, no retreat, we were to stand and hold on as long as we could, or as long as we lasted – not a very rosy thought![1]

1 The 21st September was a trying day for the 7th KOSB in the northern part of the perimeter, they were coming under increasing attack. The White House seeming to bear the brunt of the attacks, and so he ordered the removal of the RAP to a house outside the immediate fighting area. This is what the RMO Captain B Devlin recalled some years later: 'In the afternoon the RAP was threatened by a German 88 mm gun, so my CO ordered me to remove the wounded to another house, about 200 yards away on the opposite side of the road. This I seem to remember was a fairly narrow suburban residential street. At the far end of the street was a crossroad or T-junction. Here we believed was an enemy sniper. I set off, carrying a large Red Cross flag suspended between two poles, at the head of a column, some walking,

A Hamilcar and two Horsa gliders after being released over the Rhine. On the left of the
picture are some of the houses of the village of Heelsum
(Airborne Museum 'Hartenstein', Oosterbeek)

We didn't know our position then, but what was left of the Division was now
in a half-circle, with the River Rhine at the bottom and the remnants took up a defence in that half-circle, with Div. HQ roughly in the centre, about half a mile behind our positions. Our position was near the outside of that perimeter. The name
of the district was Oosterbeek.

some on stretchers. When it was too late to turn back a whole Platoon (so it seemed)
of SS soldiers became evident, not just one sniper. And so we were all taken prisoner
and marched to a prisoner of war cage, where I was separated from my RAP staff
and taken with the wounded to the Municipal Hospital at Arnhem.'

35

Friday, 22nd September 1944

Four of us moved into the garden between two houses and started digging slit trenches. Dawn was now breaking. I started digging under a small tree – I felt reluctant to dig up all the flowers, cabbages, etc. The door of the cottage opened and an old man peered out with a scared look in his eyes, a younger man with him. I motioned him to get an axe to cut the roots and he brought one. I made motions for the time – he said '7.00 am' He then said 'Americanisch?' – I said 'No! Englander'. He nodded and closed the door.

The old folk were beginning to hurry away down the street, hardly knowing which way to go. I think Jerry must have got to know where we were from some of those people, for just about that time those infernal mortars opened on us again. A start of the everlasting shower of mortar bombs that were to last until we finally withdrew, three days and nights later.

We dug our small slit trenches as fast as we could and finally got below ground level – then we sat back and had a breather. I looked up at the small tree above me and – lo and behold! – it was full of small apples. I stood up and grabbed as many as I could and ate and ate. When we couldn't reach any more, we knocked the branches with our rifles.

One of the boys was round the back garden, he whispered quietly that he had found peaches. I said I would be right there, but before I could move I heard a fairly distant shot and he dashed round the corner. A sniper had taken a shot at him – 'So, they had got our positions already, had they?'

Well, we expected a few hours respite at least, but we got none. Jerry was evident – by bringing in more men and closing round us. Each time one of the Orderly men passed we asked what was the news – 'Where was the Army?' – 'How long were we to last here?' – 'Why didn't Monty get through?' If those men knew the answers, they never told us. The CO was the same, he knew our position from meetings at our Div. HQ with the Div. Commander, General Urquhart, but never once did he let on that we were in such a desperate position. He came round regularly and told us all sorts of things to keep our spirits up. At first he said we shouldn't have to hold out more than 24 hours at most – we thought 'Well, we can do that alright!'

Mortar bombs were coming down heavily, I lay in the trench and listened to the dull Boom! Boom! Boom! and then listened for the sighing whistle of the bombs – we could soon tell how near they were going to drop. As Jerry found our true positions, so he plastered us more, but what was worse, his snipers were closing in and making any movement above ground practically impossible.

The short street down the village was free from snipers as yet. At the top end of the street there was open ground and woods opposite and at the lower end the houses were held or covered by men of the Glider Pilot Regt. – these men suffered heavy casualties in the next few days. We still had one Carrier left and this was kept busy running from one position to another with ammunition and what rations we had left, mostly for the wounded.

The small village hall on the opposite side of the road to us was made into a First Aid Post, although medical supplies were nil. I guess all the staff could do was to change field dressings as they became soaked in blood and probably give a little morphia to ease the pain. Outside the wall they hung a white sheet with a red 'X' painted with blood on it. This was maybe a good sign for the snipers, but those mortar bombs didn't take any notice of any red cross flag – and so the small RAP had to take it's chance along with the rest. Strangely enough it was never hit by a direct shot.

The sound of 'planes again – fighters! We hoped they were ours, but no! The next second I heard the rattle of their cannons and machine guns. They flashed over the house-tops, guns blazing, and I wondered where the RAF were – where were all those Spitfires, Mustangs and Typhoons they had told us about? They strafed from one position to another and then flew off once more. Strangely enough the time was again about 10.00 in the morning, when our supply 'planes were due.

Our 'planes did not come for another two hours or more. As before, we couldn't mistake the increasing roar of those hundreds of engines, together with the Flak, tearing them out of the sky. I watched for them coming into view, then they passed over our heads as before, hundreds of coloured parachutes dropping down from the sky – if only hundreds of Paratroops would drop!

A Stirling roared over our heads only 100-200 ft up, engines and wing were blazing – a few seconds later we heard a dull crash in the distance. Most of the supplies were dropping to Jerry as before – it grieved us to see those men risking their lives and machines to drop supplies to Jerry. Even more ironical that we were being bombed with our own mortar bombs and shot with our own guns and bullets!

I sat back in my trench and looked to the now quiet sky. I looked to a small patch of blue and while those mortar bombs dropped all round I prayed – a simple prayer asking for His help, 'Give us help' – 'Send reinforcements for us' – that was my prayer.

Two men were needed to go to a Company position, Bob and Henry went out, leaving two of us together. All the time I was there I always remembered little things we had been taught to remember. Whenever I was looking out of a slit trench or window I kept moving my head from one position to another, in case some sniper was trying to get a 'bead' on me. Whenever I crossed the open I did so in double quick time, and when I ran along the street I ran from side to side slightly, in a zigzag – it was those little things that often made the difference between life and death.

I had many thoughts to myself in the trench – I wondered how it would end. 'I expect it will be in the papers back home – Mum and Dad will be wondering where I am, if I am alright'. I thought if we are wiped out it will be in the papers at home, how we stood our ground and died – 'We would probably be heroes when the story is told'. 'If I am killed, how will Mum take it?' I pictured the telegram reaching home. All those things ran through my mind as I listened to those mortar bombs sighing down, exploding all around, feeling as if each one was coming into my back.

There was a steady flow of men into the First Aid Post opposite, some walking, most on stretchers – I wondered where they were putting them all.

I didn't have a very good field of view from that slit trench as the hedge and gardens came within 20 ft. of me at one side, so that I had to be constantly on the alert. There was no definite line between us and the Germans. Our boys were crawling about the gardens and sniping from houses, and Jerry was doing the very same, so that when we heard a noise in the garden or in a house, we listened and watched with finger on trigger to see who it was.

We had still managed to hold on to a Vickers machine gun and our boys did wonders with it – all day long that Vickers was chattering away, keeping Jerry down under cover. It also gave us heart to hear it pumping lead – we could recognise our guns from Jerry's.

Jerry still kept up that awful crackle of explosive bullets over our heads – they weren't too dangerous, but the continual noise had an unnerving effect. He was also using his famous 88 mm guns against us now. These guns fired with a terrific crack and screech combined and all we heard of the shell was 'Shzipp!' and then the bang of it exploding.

I thought of our position and what we were up against. We were now only a handful of men, hundreds instead of thousands, dozens instead of hundreds. We had rifles, a few Sten guns, fewer PIAT guns and bombs, practically no mortars or bombs, no Artillery guns, no Anti-Tank guns, in fact practically everything was finished except for our own small weapons – rifles and revolvers.

What had we against us? Hundreds, probably thousands of German Infantry, mortars bombing day and night, heavy tanks, half-track armoured cars, flame-throwers, 88 mm guns and German fighters strafing every day. I smiled to myself when I thought of the odds against us – 'and yet here we are holding out still, without food, without sleep, five days and nights now!' 'How much longer was it going to last?' 'Where was Monty?' 'Why didn't they send us more men, more guns?' 'Where were all those RAF fighters we had heard about?' It just seemed as if they had forgotten us altogether. We had been left to fight and die until we were all wiped out!

'Sandy' Munro came along and we asked him our position – 'What was news?' He didn't know much, the Second Army was held up, couldn't get through to us – maybe a tank reconnaissance force will break through that night. We raised our hopes, 'Maybe in the morning our tanks would be here!' We didn't know our exact position. I thought that we were at one side of Arnhem and over the bridge Jerry was holding back our main Army, so that when the main force got through it would come over the bridge and past us into Arnhem. That was why the CO said we had to hold on to that area at all cost. I guess the main reason why we had to hold on was so that Jerry couldn't cut across our half-circle at the bottom and so cut off our one and only way of withdrawal over the river.

The day wore on, dusk came. The CO, Lt. Col. Payton Reid, came along and told us all to stand-to and be ready for an attack from Jerry. I worked my rifle bolt, made sure it was O.K., took out a couple of hand-grenades and lay them on the ground in front of me and then waited, watching the road and gardens. I expected to see Germans come across any second – the same thoughts were running through my mind – 'This is it!' I resigned myself to die there, but before I went I was resolved to take some of those Jerries with me. I looked at the pins in the grenades, they were set O.K. I tried to lick my dry lips but my mouth was dry.

After the war Verlengde Paul Krugerstraat became Paul Krugerstraat and the houses were renumbered. The Regimental Aid Post at the time of the battle was at no 27 which is now no 70 (Courtesy Robert Sigmond)

Darkness came, Jerry didn't make an attack – I breathed again! 'What was wrong with Jerry?' If he made a mass attack he was sure to wipe us out, he must have thought we were strong in numbers, and I think his Infantry were a bit scared of us 'Red Devils'. They knew we were desperate, being cornered and took no prisoners. He probably thought he would finish us off with mortaring and sniping without sacrificing any more of his men, and so he didn't make a really organised attack that night, or any other night.

Somebody came along and gave us the password for the night. We thought we might get a few hours rest and hoped for reinforcements of some sort or, better still, relief from the main Army.

However, the darkness brought no respite, those infernal mortars still kept up their moaning, and it seemed like Jerry made a practice of setting fire to a house here and there so that his damned snipers could inflict their steady toll. During some of those heavy mortar barrages I lay in a small trench and said a silent prayer often, asking Him to see us through yet another night.

The darkness made us even more 'jumpy', for every shadow and every noise made me lift my rifle and watch. I crept up the garden a short way and sprinkled dry twigs on the path, so that I couldn't be surprised from that direction. Then the two of us arranged to try and get a little sleep, about one hour at a time, we couldn't keep our eyes open longer than that. We managed an hour or two, but each time a few men came along the street he would awaken me or I would awaken him and we would try to recognise the uniform in the dark, probably having to call quietly for the password.

Over in the First Aid Post we could hear some of the boys moaning terribly, one or two crying, often hearing a cry for 'Mother!' It was awful to listen to in the dark[1].

1   Over the course of the last couple of days the Germans had been increasing the ferocity of their attacks but they only made small progress in reducing the size of the 1st Airborne's perimeter. With ammunition running low, the defenders certainly made sure every shot counted. When it realised that the RMO Captain Devlin had been captured, a decision was taken by the ADMS (the Senior Medical Officer) Colonel Warrack, to send a replacement from those working in the MDS's around the crossroads in the centre of the village. The doctor selected was Captain S Kaye from the 16th Parachute Field Ambulance RAMC. His section had accompanied the 1st Parachute Battalion in the early part of the Battle and he was one of the few survivors to make it back to Oosterbeek on the 19th of September. He made it to the KOSB area on this day and it is believed the Battalion's Padre Reverend Morrison together with the RAP Sergeant, Sergeant Hyslop had set up a new RAP in a house on the Paul Krugerstraat. It was set up in Number 27 but due to a renumbering of the houses after the war it is now number 70.

36

Saturday, 23rd September 1944

In the early hours of the morning, two of our lads brought two Jerries into the trench with us – prisoners needed for interrogation. We put them in the trench between our two and made them sit with hands on top of their heads. We wanted no tricks and we told them so with the business end of a revolver – they were plenty scared of us!

Now we had to stay awake, and longed for the dawn to come – 'Would it bring our Army?' We were beginning to give up hope of being relieved, I guess. We had been told an armoured column was trying to break through and if they succeeded would be here at dawn. It raised our hopes a little to be told that. Little did we know the main Army was having a tough fight to relieve themselves 20 miles away – just as well we didn't know!

The hours wore on, mortars still blasting the houses and ground all around, surely they would run short of bombs soon, but why should they when the RAF had dropped them enough weapons and bombs to blast us for a month!

At last the sky lightened, day was coming – our prisoners were taken away. The CO came around and told us to stand-to for an expected attack. Once more I prepared with rifle and grenades, once more I expected to die. I thought of a picture I had seen at home entitled 'Each dawn I die' – what could be more fitting? With every dawn I expected it to be my last – and yet – somehow at the back of my mind I had a sort of feeling or sense that I would get back home again. I never once lost that feeling. They say when a man is going to be killed he can sense it – he knows he is. Well, I guess I had that feeling that I wasn't going to be killed.

The same routine again started, watching and waiting for Jerry to attack, mortar bombs dropping, 88 mm shells 'Shzipping' over, and the never-ending 'snap' of the snipers.

Of course, this wasn't the same story in other parts of that perimeter, for in other sectors Jerry was attacking, but our boys were killing four of them to one of ours. However, our losses were very bad and those that were left couldn't hold on much longer. Even at the top of the street near the woods our boys were holding them back all the time, their rifles and Brens were never quiet, but in my small area it wasn't quite so desperate.

The firing was very heavy in the gardens behind us, I knew some of our Company boys were out there and so I didn't worry too much, I knew it was them and I thought there were plenty of them to hold out. Our Sergeant came along and asked us to come with him to have a look around the gardens and sheds to see if any Jerries had got amongst us in the dark. We started at one end and searched every shed and garden on both sides of our street, but it was O.K. I dropped back into my foxhole – I didn't feel too safe up on top of the ground – I expected a bullet every second!

I was sitting in the trench when 'Shzipp', and the ground dug up just a few feet away and something rattled onto the road. I looked and there lay an 88 mm shell unexploded! I guess my number wasn't on that one – if it was, I was lucky.

Jerry, as usual, was methodical in his mortaring just as he was in other things. He would plaster the area at the top of the road for about ¼ hour without a break, then a spell of a ½ minute or so while they re-aimed, and then the next ¼ hour barrage would be on Div. HQ behind. Another spell, then I crouched low, face to the ground for I knew it was our turn next. I heard the 'thuds' of the mortars firing and then they showered all around us. I thought to myself, 'In barrages like these it's only a matter of time before a guy gets killed, it's a sure thing that one would hit him sooner or later!'

Normally, at the front, the Infantry don't have to stand up to a pounding such as we took, for Artillery support or tanks can very often be called in, but that was not so with us – we just had to take it. I knew those mortar barrages were terrific while I was there, and when I finally got back home I read that in those barrages 15 bombs a minute were dropped on us continuously. A bomb every 4 seconds for hours at a time for 4 days and nights – that was what practically broke my nerve!

A Signal Corporal came along and asked one of us to go with him for mortar or PIAT bombs from the Rifle Company across the gardens. I followed after him, he crouched low, running from house to house, and then round the back gardens we went. We came to a garden surrounded by a high hedge and wire, we went round by a shed, a shot fired, we dashed back again!

I went round the side of the house, I stepped into the door, two of our boys were in the passage, one badly wounded and bleeding, the other lad was trying to bandage him. He jumped when I hopped into the door. I greeted him the usual way – 'How're you doing, fella?' 'Are there any snipers around?', I asked. 'Yes, some over there somewhere' he pointed. I had a quick look outside again. The Corporal was calling quietly to come with him. I ran after him, in that low crouching run one gets into in action.

At the bottom of the garden we came to a hedge and wire fence. The Corporal leapt over, it was a bit high for me – I hesitated a second, a bad thing to do – then I threw my rifle over the hedge and dived over after it. I landed flat on the other side as a shot sounded, if it was at me, I was lucky again!

I grabbed my rifle and ran across to where our boys were. Some of the mortar boys were in a shallow pit with a couple of mortars. I recognised Joe Steele, he laughed when he saw me land on my face. 'How's things, Joe?' I called as I went past. 'Enjoying yourself?' he asked.

I ran on and into a big shed behind a house. They had a few spare PIAT bombs there. We took two cartons each, three bombs in each carton. I picked up a .38 revolver – no, a .45 it was, for I tried to scrounge some ammunition for it, I remember. I tucked it in my smock front and then away we went again. We had the same dodging about to get back, finally running up the street to where the CO was sitting with a couple of Officers, and dumped the bombs down by the house.

I ran over the road to the First Aid Post – I went round the back, the first thing I saw was the concrete path covered in blood. A couple of blood-soaked stretchers were propped by the wall. In a small shed were the rifles and ammunition taken from the wounded, I couldn't find any revolver ammunition. I picked up a rifle in good working order and well oiled. I looked on the floor and saw a bullet-proof vest the same as I had on. It had a jagged bullet-hole in it – I didn't feel so confident in mine now!

I sat on some logs, the mortar bombs were still blasting all around, I was just about dead-beat – tired, hungry and nerves shaken. An Orderly came round, he looked at me, I guess he could see I was just about all-in. He asked if I was O.K. I said 'Yes, but hellish hungry!' He came back with a bit of meat and vegetables on a plate that someone had left. I wolfed it down, it sure tasted good to me.

After a few minutes I went out again, I glanced at the back garden, I saw lads laid out there close together. I guess they couldn't do any more for them – not even a blanket to cover them.

I dived back into the slit trench, the mortars were dropping closer than usual. I crouched low in the trench, a couple of bombs burst on the house nearby, another one on the ground closer, a shower of dirt fell on me. I lost my nerve a bit – I jumped out and ran up the road towards the green at the top. 'Sandy' Munro was in a trench in a garden. He said 'What's wrong, bombed out?' I forced a grin and said 'No, I'm going for water'.

The house at the top of the street had a pump in it. I hesitated at the gate, something seemed to make me turn away and I ran across to an empty trench a few yards away. I dived in, one of the boys was in the next trench and I asked him what things were like up there. He said 'There's a sniper over there somewhere and plenty of mortars'. Just then a bomb landed plumb onto the house I had been going to go into for water – I was lucky!

I lay for a while and waited for the mortars to ease off a little and then I scrambled out and ran back to my old foxhole. It was still there – I quite expected to see it blown to Hell – but no! It seemed like someone was looking after me .... I wondered!

The firing across the gardens was getting heavier now. Jerry was closing in and bringing in more men. Every so often I could hear the Germans shouting to each other and making screams. I guess it was for two reasons. Firstly, to give them confidence and false courage and secondly, to make us believe there were a great number of them and break our nerve. I must admit it didn't do the nerves any good to hear them and be unable to see them in the woods and undergrowth. It didn't actually break our nerves to hear them – it sort of maddened us. We lay there with fingers on triggers and mumbling something like 'Come on out, you blasted, b****y square-heads!' It made us feel like jumping up and sorting them out. That was just what he wanted us to do – it was what was called 'Psychological Warfare' and Jerry was a master at it.

Some of our boys came from the gardens and past us so I asked them who they were. 'D Company' they replied. I asked if the rest were still out there and they said 'No, we're the lot!' I was a bit shaken – a handful of men were a 'Company'. Now I really knew how many men we had lost!

I got ready for any surprise – all of a sudden two figures in grey-green dashed out from behind the house in front of us. They saw us at the same time as we saw them. Before I could pull the trigger they dashed back. I fired just as they disappeared again – the shot probably scared them anyway – I didn't see them again.

A sniper was on the road now and things were pretty warm, we could hardly show our heads at all. The CO came along regularly and tried to keep our spirits high. He said 'Don't be afraid of all the noise from Jerry, there's only 20-30 of them, there's enough of us to hold them'. I thought 'If that's the case, why don't we attack and wipe them out?' but I guess the position was not as the CO would have us believe. He told us again that if we could hold out for another night we would very probably be relieved at dawn. Whether he knew the real position or not I don't know, but I do know he was a soldier, he would have held out there until he didn't have a man left, but he wouldn't have moved without orders.

Even in a spot like that, our boys still had their sense of humour and kept a wonderful spirit. Most of the Company boys were in two's and three's and they regularly passed across the gardens crouched low and making whooping noises like Red Indians. I had to laugh when I heard them, what lads they were – no wonder the Germans couldn't understand us and thought us mad.

I guess the RAF had given us up for a bad job, they didn't come any more. They had done their best and they had done a good job and their losses had been very heavy – I took off my hat to those men.

We cursed a little amongst ourselves, the thought of being deserted, left in a hell-hole like that made us bitter towards our leaders back home. We asked dozens of questions amongst ourselves – 'Why didn't they get through to us?' 'Why didn't they send us a few thousand Paratroops?' We just couldn't realise that Operation Arnhem was a glorious failure. If possible it could only mean one thing before long – withdrawal before we were all wiped out, but as there was no talk of withdrawal, we could only come to the conclusion that it was to be a stand to the end, and for such we resigned ourselves.

Another day wore on, snipers, mortars and fatigue wearing us down. Dusk began to fall again and we stood-to for yet another attack. Complete darkness came and Jerry didn't attack, but as usual he set fire to a house here and there to light things up.

Two of our stretcher-bearers were going out for wounded and they needed four men for a 'cover party'. I went with them – we made our way up to the top of the road and asked some of the boys where the wounded were. They pointed in the direction of the small building they were in. We made off across the open ground crouching low, on our left were woods and fields – and snipers. On our right was the dull glow of the burning houses. Lucky for us there was a shallow dip in the field, we hugged this dip.

We found the small brick building behind a house and cautiously listened. I called quietly if anyone was there and a voice in the pitch dark said 'Yes, two of us'. We crouched down outside, the stretcher-bearers went in, groping in the dark. They called for us to help, so I went inside. I put my foot down on something soft so I stooped down and felt – it was somebody's leg I had stood on! He hadn't made a noise, so I guessed he was dead.

I felt my way over to the wounded lad, the lads whispered for me to lift his legs. I touched his legs, he jumped and cried not to touch his legs, he had got it in the thighs. I said 'I can't help it, old pal, you'll have to bear it for a minute'. I took hold of his legs, lifted, he moaned and nearly screamed in pain. I didn't have to take any notice. I stumbled back to the door, once more stepping on the dead body of someone. We got him out of the door. He was moaning pitifully and asking for water. We had none and I told him to keep quiet for a few minutes and we would get him to the FAP – then he would get a good drink of warm tea (what a hope!).

There was a noise of somebody coming, we froze still, he still cried for water – I felt like holding my hand over his mouth. If these were Germans he would give away our position. It was half a dozen of our boys patrolling for Jerries. The CO was with them, they moved round the house, then there was a burst of firing. I crouched back to the wall – we couldn't go out yet, there were Jerries snooping around.

I watched a shadow in the hedge, I thought I saw it move – the more I stared at it in the dark, the more it looked like a German. I stood close into the shadow of the wall for a few minutes, watching the shadows amongst the trees, revolver cocked and ready – nothing happened. Then the burst of shooting stopped so I said 'Come on, fella, let's go!' The other two picked up the stretcher, I moved on in front a few yards, crouched as low as possible and we started to cross the open to where our boys were.

I stopped suddenly and lifted my hand for them to halt. I could see a dark shadow on the ground in front. I moved up cautiously, then I could see that by the way he was laying, face down, hands in front, that he was dead. Then I was close enough to make out the smock and familiar helmet and saw that it was one of our boys – I waved them on. That damned fire on our left made a good background for snipers, I hugged the ground closely.

About 60 ft. from our boys I thought I had better go on myself and tell them it was our lads coming, for if some of those lads saw figures crawling in the dark, they would surely open up on us. When I got close enough, I called in a low whisper 'Friend' and then told them two more were coming over with a stretcher. I went back again and called low for them to come on over. We got the wounded round to the First Aid Post. The Padre, who was acting Medical Officer, took charge of the wounded and asked if we were O.K. He gave us a pat on the shoulder and away we went.

I crawled back to my foxhole and began another night of trying to keep awake, snatching a few minutes sleep from time to time. The rattle of tank tracks and the roar of their engines could be heard in the near distance. I thought 'If those things come in the morning we are finished', for by now we had no weapons to stand against those tanks. Once more we were told that our main Army might break through at dawn, once more we raised our hearts, I believe once more I prayed.

Those infernal mortars were still dropping regularly, first one area, then another. I guess it was just to keep us from sleeping, but we were too tired and dead-beat to bother about them now. Often during a barrage I would lay in the bottom of the trench and close my eyes and often I would give a start and open my eyes to find that I was dropping off to sleep.

37

Sunday, 24th September 1944

The dawn came at last, but no sign of any relief. We were to go through yet another day – another day of mortars, snipers, shells, hunger and tiredness. How long was this to last? How long did they think we could last? I guess we could have got food from the cellars of some of the houses, but somehow I felt reluctant to loot the food from these Dutch people – hadn't we brought them enough trouble already!

We had now been around Arnhem for a week, holding out against odds that were never planned for in any Airborne attack – holding out but suffering terrible casualties. In our area we now numbered a few dozen men, where once we had been hundreds. Most of our Officers had gone, Sergeants or Corporals were in charge of what men were left. A Glider pilot had joined the CO to act as sort of Second in Command[1]. The old CO was still on the move, all day long he seemed to be here and there, with his revolver in his hand. I heard when I returned home that he was wounded many times, but he never showed it.

It was raining steadily, the bottoms of the trenches were muddy and wet, rifles were clogged with mud, as before. I had a tin of water and kept swilling the bolt of the rifle to clear the mud. No sooner had I got it working and put it on top, when it would clog up again. I got hold of two more rifles and loaded each one and lay them on top of the trench – that was three shots I'd have anyway!

One of our Corporals, Bob Sweetman, came along. Before we could say anything, he started to run across the road. We shouted 'Look out, Bob!'. The same instant he hesitated, a shot sounded – he fell face down. He looked up at us with a surprised look in his eyes. He dragged himself nearer to us and one of the boys held out a rifle for him to hold and pulled him into the side of the house. Two of the boys were fumbling around him, then one said 'He's dead!' – just like that. One minute he was with us, the next minute he was laid face down on the ground – dead! He was a good lad, another one of the best. Nobody touched him, he just lay there with the rain soaking into him.

I felt bitter, how useless it all seemed, good boys dying out here – for what purpose? We had lost our objective, why weren't we withdrawn days ago? The snipers were now closing all around us, we couldn't raise our heads at all. Some of our lads

---

1   This Glider Pilot was Sergeant Tilley from E Squadron of the GPR, he had flown a Horsa on the first lift with a jeep and trailer and six men of Support Company and had stayed with the Battalion since landing on LZ S. This is what the Padre Reverend Morrison later recalled about Sergeant Tilley: 'I remember Sergeant Tilley well, he was an unforgettable character. How he came in contact with the CO in the first place I don't know, but he appointed himself as his bodyguard during the last few days of the Battle. He came round the RAP from time to time and went around cheerfully telling everyone that if they just held on for a few hours more, XXX Corps would arrive. He was certainly a tower of strength and boosted morale wherever he went. His confidence and enthusiasm were infectious.'

Cpl. Bob Sweetman's grave 2004. Died 25th September 1944 aged 28, buried in Arnhem Oosterbeek War Cemetery – 21.A.12 – N.B. Date incorrect on his gravestone (Editor's collection)

were in the house next to us. I said to Davidson in the next hole 'When I shout RIGHT, jump out and get into that house.' He said 'O.K.'. I grabbed my rifle and out I went and into the house.

There were about five others in there. We stood by the windows and rested a while. There was a large hamper of apples in the room, so we started to eat those. I got the boys to drag a chest of drawers up behind the door, to stop any bullets and told them to watch the windows. Two of us went into the other room and squatted by the window there.

A Sergeant came in and told us to get organised a bit, somebody to go upstairs. I grabbed a rifle and said I'd have a look around, so up the stairs I went and cautiously looked out over the gardens. I couldn't see a sign of anybody, then I thought I saw someone move in the trees. I took aim and fired. The next second a heavy machine gun or cannon let fly at my room, 2 inch holes bore right through the wall and out the other side. I flattened to the floor – 'That's done it!' I said to myself. I went downstairs in two jumps and said to the boys 'The Hell with that, it's suicide up there!' and I went back to the room.

It was now fairly dark, the boys were all dead-beat and fed-up. One or two were asleep on the floor. Davidson and I went upstairs again and he lay on a single bed, I lay down on the floor. I just lay a while and listened – not a sound, no firing. I thought to myself 'What if everybody goes and leaves us here'. I heard a few footsteps along the road, suppose they were Jerries! Maybe our boys had got through to us! I looked out the window and I heard a few words in English.

At that the firing started again, mortars and machine guns. I said 'I'm going down out of this'. Downstairs I went – the rest of the boys were squatted around, some in the doorway to the cellar. One or two bullets came through the door and hit the wall. We moved down the steps of the cellar and it was then I received a big shock, for down that small cellar were all the Dutch family! An old Grannie was sitting there, two or three men, two women and three or four kids – I was amazed! All that week those people had been in that cellar, while we fought on top. We tried to speak to them a bit.

All of us were now on the cellar steps, we were all about at an end. Somebody suggested trying to sneak out into Arnhem to the bridge where we thought our main Army was. We got the old man to sketch us the way to the railway and then into Arnhem. The boys said that we had best put all our guns on top of the stairs, for if any Jerries came in now they would probably throw down a couple of hand grenades and kill the old people as well. We did this – I wasn't caring much any more. Some of the boys took their Dutch money from their pockets and gave it to the old Grannie, we said it was no use to us now.

One of our Sergeants was on top of the cellar steps. After a while he went out and I guess he must have told the CO, for not long after we heard the voice of the CO coming in through a window. We grabbed our guns and stumbled into the room again – discipline showing itself. He gave us a bawling out and told us to get to the windows and barricade them, we were going to hold out there to the last!

'Well', I thought, 'that's that – we've had it now!' and started barricading the windows with anything we could find. I piled a mattress and table against the small window, leaving a small space to watch through. At the big window we dragged the chest, wardrobe and chairs – it wasn't meant to be bullet-proof, but to stop any grenades from 'lobbing in'.

The dawn was breaking again. The CO came round once more to see what we were doing – he was satisfied to see us standing by the window spaces. He told someone to go upstairs and snipe from up there. Once more he told us, 'We would probably be relieved later in the day or during the night. In any case, we were not to leave these few houses, for if they did get through to us they would come through this place and so we had to hold on'. He told us to be ready for a Jerry attack at dawn. I thought 'If he does attack, it won't be long before we've all had it, for as soon as he located our exact position he would mortar us flat!'

We stood and waited – I stood by the window, revolver ready, rifle standing by the wall. Nothing happened apart from the ceaseless mortaring. I thought, 'Surely there's nothing left of our Div. HQ.', for the day before Jerry had mortared that place for 2½ hours without a break. As I listened to the bombs whistling over, I pictured what it was like over there where they were dropping – I knew it must have been wicked[2].

2   During the period 22nd to 24th September the Battalion slightly reduced the area it held, basically due to dwindling numbers. The Battalion was a mere shadow of the body that had left the UK just a few days before. From the 765 or so men who left on 17th September only around 120 were left. The positions each roughly held by a group of 30 men were as follows:
B Company for an area around the junctions of Steijnweg and Bothaweg
C Company for an area around the junctions of Bothaweg and Oranjeweg
D Company for an area around the junctions Oranjeweg and Paul Krugerstraat

Lieutenant John Howe, commander of the 1st Border's No.25 Anti-Tank Platoon, lying on a stretcher mounted on the front of a British Jeep, being evacuated from Oosterbeek during the truce of Sunday 24th September. He is accompanied by a British soldier, sitting in the passenger seat, and a German driver
(Copyright: Imperial War Museum BU1102)

38

Monday, 25th September 1944

Well, another Monday – how different from last Monday! We now knew we couldn't last much longer – a couple of days at most. The usual sniping carried on, only now they had us well covered, we didn't see anybody out in the open, only the occasional one or two would dive from house to house.

The main body of us were barricaded in 3 houses, about eight or ten in each house. I thought, 'Well, I'm still alive and in the last few, I'm lucky to be here at all!' I looked outside the window to the soaked body of Bob. 'If only I could get over there, I could grab the water bottle and Bob might have an iron ration in his pocket – he might also have some cigarettes in his pocket – if only I could get to him!' However the snipers were too deadly.

One of our Canadian Officers came in and asked how things were. We started grousing about our position – 'Why didn't they send us more Paratroops? – Why didn't they try to help us?' I guess he didn't know any more than we did. He said 'Somebody had better go upstairs and watch from there' and after a while he went out again[1].

We stood by the windows, watching, waiting, all day, wondering why Jerry didn't attack – he must have still been scared of us 'Red Devils'. His Fighters came over and gave us some more cannon shells to be going on with, but still his Infantry didn't attack.

One of our young Officers ran over to us and had a look around. He asked me how many rounds I had for my revolver. I replied 'Six – how many have you got?' 'About the same' he replied. I turned back to the window. 'What a Hell of a spot to be in!' I said. 'Hmm, not much we can do about it' he said quietly. We talked a bit about our position in general – how the rest of the Companies were – where the other Battalions were – where the main Army was – what was our chances? He thought the same as we did, I guess.

He then said someone had better get upstairs. I was waiting for him to say that, everybody looked at him and he looked around. I guess he thought his orders didn't carry much weight in that place, so he grabbed a rifle standing by the wall and up he went. A few minutes passed, then two shots sounded upstairs. That did it! It sounded to me like Jerry blasted the top of that house with half a dozen cannon and a couple of 88's all together. The Officer came down the stairs just as I had done before him!

1 It is probably not well known that quite a number of junior officers especially in the Airlanding Battalions were Canadians. In 1943 the British high Command realised they were running short of junior infantry officers, so it was decided to ask the Canadian Government if they could help by loaning officers. The result was the CANLOAN Scheme in which over 600 Canadians served in British Infantry units. 10 of the KOSB officers at Arnhem were Canadian, of whom 2 were killed and 8 taken prisoner. It is likely the Canadian mentioned here was Lieutenant E Carter.

From then we were 'on the spot' in that house, Jerry tore at the roof with incendiary or tracer bullets and set it well and truly alight. Well, where to now? The snipers would be waiting for us – they were!

We hung on a while longer. We told the old people to clear out. I sure felt sorry for Grannie. It was coming in dark again so I told the lad with me that I was making a dash for it. He said 'O.K.' and we grabbed a rifle each. I opened the door and dived over the garden and into a slit trench. We raised our heads – 'Zipp!' – I ducked quickly. 'This place is no good, let's get back to the other trench' I said.

This trench was on the other side of a wire fence about 4 ft. high but this wasn't going to stop me. I suddenly jumped out and rushed at the wire fence. I threw over the rifle first and half dived over after it and carried on into the slit trench. No sooner had we got into the trench then – 'Zipp!' I heard a thud nearby, sniper again! Some of our boys were in the small cottage alongside so I called them to open the door. I jumped out again and into the house I went.

There were a couple of Officers inside with about eight men. I recognised the eyes and voice of Johnny McGurk. His face, like ours, was just a black, whiskered mask. I gave him a little laugh. 'How're you doing, Johnny?' I asked. 'Not bad' he replied.

It was now quite dark and we had to be dead silent in case any Jerry was listening outside. Every few minutes one of the boys would drop off to sleep and begin to snore, so somebody else would stumble across and shake him. We stood around in the pitch dark watching the windows – the firing had eased off a bit now.

Somebody said there were jars of fruit in the cellar. I went down – the Officers had a small candle burning. There was a wounded lad laid on the floor, he had a bullet through his face and head – we got him out a few minutes later. I opened some of the jars of preserved apples and pears and ate them for a few minutes – but didn't feel like eating – too much to think about.

39

Monday Night, 25th September 1944
Withdrawal

One of the Officers dashed in, he said, 'We are pulling out at 9.00 pm. We are to make for the river and get over to the main Army'. I couldn't believe that we were to get back to the main Army. I thought of the waiting snipers and machine guns outside – I didn't think much to our chances. He told us all to get strips of blanket to muffle our feet. Somebody brought down a white blanket and we each cut off strips. We got these round our boots and I darkened mine with some sort of juice I found, then stood around waiting.

We had no idea of the route – the Officers said they had an idea of the way we had to go. The firing had died down now, it was ominously quiet outside – it seemed like Jerry was waiting for our next move. The minutes drew on and the Officer kept giving the minutes out. 'Ten to go!' 'Seven!' 'Is everybody ready?' 'I'm going to throw out a grenade first, then dash!' 'Five minutes!' 'Two minutes!' 'Get ready!' 'Right! Open up!' He threw out a grenade – a few seconds – Bang! – and out we went – across the road and between two walls behind the house.

It seemed like Jerry had been waiting for this signal, for at this minute he opened up with everything – mortars, shells, machine guns – tracers streamed across the gardens – it seemed like an impossibility to cross those gardens.

We waited a few minutes; the two Officers were in front. One of the boys, Johnny, took hold of his smock tail, I took hold of his, about four more followed me – I don't know what happened to the rest of them[1].

'Let's go!' they said, and we ran across the gardens, crouched low, stumbling. The whole place was lit up by flares – Jerry certainly knew we were making a break and he was just as determined to stop us. We came onto a street and turned right, hugging the garden hedge.

We strode over a couple of dead bodies, turned left into a big garden – wrong way! Out again – up the street – left again. Lucky for us we did, we ran into the lawn of a large house, what had been Div. HQ

---

1   Due to the fact that XXX Corps had been unable to reach the south bank of the Rhine opposite Driel in any strength, permission was given in the morning of the 25th for the survivors of the 1st Airborne to cross the river. General Urquhart called it Operation Berlin and designed his plan on the successful evacuations from Gallipoli in 1915 and 1916 which he had studied when a student at Staff College. The evacuation went relatively successfully with over 2,000 either swimming across or being ferried by Engineers from XXX Corps. However the cost of Arnhem to the 1st Airborne was high, around 1,400 had been killed and 6,500 taken prisoner (many taken before the formation of the Oosterbeek perimeter). At the 7th KOSB roll call on the morning of the 26th in Nijmegen just 74 people were present.

Flares were going up continuously – shells and bombs were bursting across the lawn, each time one burst we dropped flat. I was still near to Johnny and each time we dropped I said 'Are you O.K.?' 'Yes, are you?' came the reply.

Strange but I didn't feel too scared, probably thinking too much, remembering to drop with every flash of a shell. I didn't know what to think of the terrific bombardment – personally I thought our boys had got through and we were running into a pitched battle between them and Jerry.

It seemed like we were heading straight into Jerry – we were, had we known! We now had the big house on our right, it seemed like Jerry was on the other side. Each time a flare went up, we froze still in the bushes, while tracers slashed across the garden. This was suicide! I said 'Come on Johnny, let's get into this house and lay low for a while.' The Officers were at a loss now, the same as us. They finally climbed into the room window and we followed after them.

The place was a shambles inside, we fumbled across the floor and lay down by the wall. We talked quietly – 'What was the use?' – 'We might as well pack in!' Mortars and shells were blasting everywhere. I thought 'It's only a matter of minutes, then they'll start to flatten this house.' Some of the boys were making plans to make a dash for it and Johnny asked me what we should do – I wasn't caring much any longer. I thought 'This is the end!' – I said we would wait until the firing quietened a bit and then try.

We dropped off to sleep, oblivious to the inferno outside – we must have slept for hours. Some of the boys crawled away during the night – I wasn't caring, I slept again.

40

Tuesday Morning, 26th September 1944

Surrender

It was broad daylight when finally we all stood up and took in our surroundings. It had once been a lovely country mansion – now it bore the signs of a week of battle – bullet marks, mortar bombs scars, broken windows and smashed furniture. The floor of the big room was covered over with packs, haversacks and equipment – abandoned by the men who had left before us and were now either over the river or dead on the banks.

We looked out across the field and lawns – there was no sign of any Germans – everything looked so peaceful. I sat on a settee and glanced at some photographs, my back was fully exposed to the wide window – and also exposed to the hidden Germans, had I known! Probably some of them actually had me in their sights, but I still lived.

The two Officers were still with us, two Lieutenants. We asked them what they thought – we made a few suggestions to them. Finally they said 'Get hold of something white and go outside and leave your guns.' A couple of boys did so – nothing happened. We all went outside and stood out on the lawn. Little did we know that machine guns were trained on us, but for some reason they did not fire. I think the

Editor, Maggie Clifton (Albert's daughter), presenting an extract (this chapter) and a photograph of Albert to J Verheij and Berry de Reus, Conservator of the Airborne Museum, Hartenstein, 26th September2004, exactly 60 years later
(Editor's collection)

reason was that these Germans were still scared of the 'Red Devils'. They were afraid to give away their position in case we decided to fight and also they didn't know how many there were of us and so were afraid of being outnumbered, a prospect the German didn't like in battle.

So we stood there and talked a bit. The Lieutenant took out his compass and pointed to the general direction of the river. I suggested that we make our way to the river and perhaps be able to get back even yet, lucky for us we didn't try it!

We heard someone coming over the lawn, it was a Civvy with a Red Cross band on his arm. He motioned for some of our boys to go with him. A few minutes later they came back carrying one of our Sergeants, badly shot in the legs. He had been shot down by those streams of bullets that we had tried to get past.

We got a bed mattress from the house and lay him on this, then another one was brought back and another mattress was brought for him. He was in terrible pain so we gave him morphia, but it didn't do much good.

A few minutes later we had a big surprise – over the field a figure stood up in full view …. A figure in grey-green! He waved us over, so we looked at the Officers. 'Come on!' they said. We started to cross the field towards him. I thought to myself, 'When they get us in the open they will probably mow us all down' – once again I resigned myself to die there. When we got near to the hedge we then saw the other Germans, laying in slit trenches. They had been laying there all the time, guns trained on us and we had not known it.

The Germans lined us up and two of them searched us for weapons. They asked if there were any more in the house. We told them only two wounded. Two of the boys went back with a German to bring them. I had a look at the Germans, they were a fairly poor lot, ragged, badly-clothed, shivering with cold, but they had plenty of guns, which we lacked – every German had one or two of our guns beside his own. Sten guns, revolvers and British hand grenades hanging on their belts. Then, in the trees, I saw what had been doing the shelling the night before – a heavy tank, it's gun pointing ominously to the big house. A good thing for us we hadn't tried to get away!

The Germans got a bit talkative – asked about England, asked us about the 'Flieger bombens' – the flying bombs. Was it right 'London kaput?' We smiled a bit, 'No!' we said 'London not kaput!' They didn't know the truth, only what they were told. They thought the South of England and London were bombed into submission by the flying bombs. I don't think they even knew the main Army was only 8 or 10 miles away. We asked them for a cigarette and chocolate – they gave us a 'Players' and a bit of 'Cadburys Chocolate' – our own supplies that had dropped to them.

We were still not sure what would happen to us, for it would be quite easy for them to machine gun us there in the woods – who would be any wiser? I thought to myself, 'If we are shot here, I suppose in time our Army will find us and the Germans would be found out and be in turn tried and shot. That wouldn't have done me any good, but it was just one of those trains of thought when a man faces death.

Well, after a while the Germans lined us up and marched us off. There were about 12 of us and the two Lieutenants. We had to carry the wounded on the mattresses, taking turn about. The Germans were plenty scared of our bombers and fighters. Time and again the guards asked us if the bombers were coming this morning. We told them 'No, they were finished.' However, when a 'plane was heard in the distance they would look up and around, we could practically see the fear in their eyes. Yes, Sir! They were plenty scared of the RAF.

As we passed through the woods we didn't see any more German Infantry. There had only been that handful around us – but what beat us were those damned mortars and tanks, we couldn't fight those things with rifles and revolvers. All around us in the woods were the signs of that week of battle. A burnt-out car, a blown-up tank, a dead German here and there, a rifle standing by a filled-in trench with an Airborne helmet on top.

Our Officers asked the Germans if we could have a few tins of food and biscuits from one of the many parachute hampers amongst the trees – these woods were littered with our supplies, coloured parachutes hanging from the trees. A German despatch rider came along on one of our motorbikes – how ironical war was, the Germans fighting and killing our boys with their own weapons!

We trudged on for maybe 2 miles. The wounded made the going pretty heavy. At last we came to a big country mansion that had been converted into a field hospital, a massive red 'X' was painted on the roof. We carried the wounded up to the door, where a Doctor came out and had a look at them, he told us to carry them inside.

It was with a certain amount of satisfaction that I noticed the place was so full of Germans that we couldn't get any further than the entrance. I glanced through the windows as we went back – that place was sure full of Germans!

We were taken around the side to a small shed where we were lined up and thoroughly searched, any valuables being taken from us. Then we sat around and watched a couple of Germans cleaning a machine gun, an ominous sign, perhaps?

After an hour or so we were again marched off – back through the woods and onto the main road where we passed the railway crossing at Wolfheze. I looked over it, only a week ago we were riding down this very road in Jeeps, strong in numbers, spirits high – and now here we were passing along in a very different way. The Dutch civilians were again stood by their houses, but now they didn't show any sign of recognition or happiness, they daren't!

We reached the main Arnhem road and then turned right towards Ede, a small town about 10 miles up the road. This road was typically continental, cobblestones instead of the usual tarmac we had at home. All along the roadside were the loveliest, picturesque bungalows and houses I've ever seen. There were some really beautiful homes, some showing signs of battle, others intact and inhabited.

Along the road we again passed the small mounds of earth with either a German or Airborne helmet hanging on top. We passed by a burnt wreck of an Army bus, a little further along we could see 3 or 4 German trucks in the wood, they had also been on fire. All along this main road there were signs of the fighting that had been going on for the past week. Our boys had certainly had some 'fun' and had obviously shown the Germans what good fighting really was – and I reckon the Germans now knew that it was not only them who could fight.

Fighter 'planes came droning over – we listened – they were ours. The German guards waved us into the side, under the trees. We lay there on the grass for a few minutes until they had passed over. We were now in a very queer position, for as we marched along these roads we were often fully exposed to our Fighter 'planes pa-

Scene at Oosterbeek: most Borderers ended up as prisoners of war
(Bundesarchiv 497/3529/18)

trolling overhead looking for just a likely target as a column of troops. Unless the light was good, the pilots couldn't possibly distinguish the colour of our uniforms and so we had to be prepared to be shot up by our own 'planes at any time.

We trudged on, mile after mile, wondering when we were to get our next meal or even a drink of water. We came to a small Dutch town so we cheered up a little and showed the people our spirit, even in defeat. We began to whistle 'Tipperary' and 'Pack up your troubles' – songs they probably remembered from other British troops in the War before us. We went on to 'Roll out the barrel', 'Lilli Marlene' and some of our latest songs.

I now noticed signs from those Dutch people as we passed by. As the people stood and looked at us, one would brush his or her hair back casually, but the fingers would be spread in a 'V'. Another would stand with legs apart in an inverted 'V'. I began to watch for all these signs and gave a wink to them as I passed. They gave no smile or sign back that the Germans could see – those people were very obviously afraid of the Germans.

We came to a small, tented German camp. We were lined up and after much shouting and bullying, two Germans began to search us. They emptied all our pockets, taking razor blades, pens, German and Dutch money and even rings from some of the boys. Another two took our names and numbers from our pay books. Then they gave us a packet containing the German version of hardtack biscuits, and believe me, they were hardtack! Biscuits made from black bread and tasting like sawdust and dog biscuit.

After a while, we were again marched off and once more began another long march – where to, we had no idea. Mile after mile we marched, and then came to another small town. As we passed through the centre of the town, the Dutch people rushed to give us a drink of water and apples. The German guards were at a loss to do anything. We all flocked around the people and took the water and apples from them that they offered to us with gratitude and thankfulness.

We formed up again and marched off once more, after we had been counted and re-counted. We trudged mile after mile, the hours dragging by. We could see our Fighter 'planes away in the distance, we watched them, so near and yet so far! From time to time we came to orchards on the roadside and we pointed to the apples. The Germans didn't hesitate, they halted us and went into the orchard. They ordered the Dutch people to give us apples, who jumped to do as they were told, once more showing their fear of the Germans.

We marched off again, wondering how long we were going to be marched? – where we were to sleep? – when were we to have a meal? It began to rain hard and very soon we were soaking wet and pretty miserable. It was also coming in dark but still we marched on and finally came to a deserted German barracks. We were marched inside and there we met many more of our boys who had been captured before us, we recognised one or two faces.

We were taken inside and shown to a big barrack room with double bunks along each side. There was no mattress of any kind on the bunks, just bare boards. We were given one old blanket each and had to make the best of it. One of the guards brought in a big milk urn full of stew and we all had to dive into this the best way we could, for as I said we had everything taken from us in the way of eating implements. We then had our first issue of German bread, it was only a small square, about 1/6th of a loaf, and a portion of lard to go with it. I didn't find the bread too bad to digest, but the sickly lard just about got the better of me.

Johnny was worse than me, he couldn't stomach the bread even, but I told him there was nothing else for it, we would have to eat it or starve and die, for there was no going to NAAFI now for supper! I had heard and read back home all about German 'ersatz butter' and so I thought this stuff like lard must be it. So I made up my mind to get it down and make the best of it.

One of our boys had managed to keep some of his toilet kit and so this was in big demand, for we all had a week's growth of beard on and were black with dirt and earth. I got a shock when I looked in the mirror, I was absolutely filthy. Only my mouth and eyes showing white. My body top was no cleaner, the earth dirt had got down my neck and the 'string vest' that I wore was filthy and had scrubbed my shoulders raw. We had a clean up the best we could and then slept two to a bunk for warmth. We were soon asleep, the first good sleep for a whole week.

41

Wednesday, 27th September 1944

We were up again at dawn, paraded and counted, then marched off again. Once more we trudged mile after mile, all day long we marched. I noticed there were no German troop concentrations anywhere and no movements of any Army vehicles on the road, which showed that the Germans had everything at the 'front' – a sort of thin ring or crust. If our Army could only break through that ring there was nothing to stop them in the rear. It made me wonder what was holding our Army up? – Why couldn't they break through? There was still a chance, I thought.

On and on we marched, heading west of all ways. It just showed how far our Airborne landing had been in front of the main Army. We finally came to the small town of Stroe, where we halted by a railway siding. We were put into a big barn for the night and given a meal of potatoes, on tin bowls, and no potatoes ever tasted better to me. We then lay in the straw the best we could to keep warm and fell off to sleep for another night, only loosening our boots and tunic necks.

42

Thursday, 28th September 1944

We were again awakened in the morning and paraded once more. Given another meal of 'spuds' and then marched out to the railway, where there was a train of goods wagons waiting. We were made to climb into these box-cars until they were chock-full – I counted 57 of us in our truck.

The small windows were closed up and the door locked and there we were in pitch darkness, with hardly room to move, let alone lay down. 57 of us herded in there like animals – no longer human beings – men. Certainly not like the young soldiers who had been the pride of the country we had only left a week or two before.

So began our journey into the heart of Holland and over the border into Germany and towards our prison camps. The beginning of a new, rather horrible, experience for most of us. An experience not one of us was to forget for the rest of our lives.

We had read in the papers back home for years about the German brutalities – prison camps – concentration camps – and now, we were to experience them ourselves.

43

Box-cars

We started on the train journey at dark, the rumours were rife. Everyone was wondering 'How long would it be?' From experience of rail journeys in Blighty we thought perhaps one or two days at the most. We sat or squatted down the best we could. It was very cold and we talked a bit at first, 'We would be O.K. in a Camp, fresh clothes, decent food etc.', – that's what we thought!

It went quiet then, each with his own thoughts. We tried to sleep, but it was difficult in such confined surroundings – our legs were on top of each other. I got cramp and somebody's boots dug into my shins, – it went on all night.

The train eventually stopped, 'Were we there?' we asked ourselves. It was all quiet for ½ hour or so and then we began moving again, we stopped again many times during the night. At last dawn showed through the cracks. 'Oh, for a drink of tea!' someone murmured. We started talking again, 'We should be there today, maybe in the morning?'

While the train was moving we inched down the small doors over the barred holes in the two opposite corners of the box-car, to drop them right down we had to prise the barbed wire off with a small penknife. Then, those who could, crowded around the holes. We watched the countryside going past, mile after mile, much like England. Most of the time the train slowed down to a crawl, 'Would it never get moving?' I thought.

The first shock during the morning was the sound of fighters! We all held our breath, the 'planes were flying low. In a few seconds I pictured cannon shells tearing through the roof, what a mess there would be! There was a roar of guns blazing, I think my heart stopped, 'This was it!' The train stopped with a jerk, we saw all the guards running for cover, how helpless we all felt – completely trapped. The roar of the 'planes passed over, 'Would they come back?' we thought. We waited for a minute or two. We thought it might have shot up the engine and somebody said 'It was a Spit chasing a Jerry', but we didn't care much, we were too relieved. Then we were on the move again, hour after hour. We never gave a thought to another horrible night such as the last one, we didn't think it would possibly happen.

Around mid-day we pulled into a siding – 'Here at last!' we said, with relief. The doors opened, but only to let out a few at a time to do what we wanted, down on the line – more relief! There were houses nearby, but we didn't have to feel any shame or embarrassment – 'Was it the German way or did they just want to humiliate us?'

A bucket of ersatz coffee came in, just lukewarm, no milk or sugar, about 7 loaves of very brown, heavy, sweet tasting bread and about 3 rolls of sausage meat, I could have eaten the whole lot myself! I kept some for later in my pocket.

We moved off again at dark … another night – 'Good grief, would I be able to put up with it and stay sane?' I thought. Another day, the same again, 'Surely no more nights?' Night again. Believe it or not, (I can't myself now), we had 6 days and nights of that to endure.

```
                                        7 KOSB,
                                        A.P.O.,
                                        England.
                                        5 Oct 44

Dear  Mrs  Blackwell,

REME  No 7622 135  Rank LCpl  Name Blackwell . A

       I regret to have to inform you that the above-named
will be officially posted as "Missing". I am writing because
it may be some little time before you receive the official
notification, and because I wish to express to you my sincere
sympathy in your anxiety, and that of all members of the
battalion.
       I am afraid that I cannot give the details of how he
came to be missing, but there were several occasions during the
operations on which complete bodies of men became cut-off and
were not seen again.  In these, and other, cases there is every
probability that the majority became prisoners of war. So,
though one can state nothing definite, there is a good
liklihood that he may be safe, though in enemy hands.
       I am sorry to be so indefinite, but thought you would
wish to hear all that is known at present. Enquiries are, of
course, on foot, and you will be informed as soon as there is
any further information.
       With renewed expressions of sympathy in your anxiety,
and trusting that we may hear more, and good news soon,


                    Yours very sincerely,


                                        Lt Col,
                              Comd 7th Bn KOSB
```

Letter to Albert's Mother from Lt. Col. Payton-Reid, 5th October 1944
(Editor's collection)

We passed through the ports of Ruhr and saw the devastation, 'How on earth was Germany holding out? I wondered. On we went through orchards, Oh, God, those apples – I craved for just one of them. I felt so weak, just lying about, with no food etc. There were many wounded men with us and we tried to get attention for them, but nothing doing.

44

The Camp

At long last we pulled into a siding and when it was our turn to get out the doors opened. I jumped down and fell straight on the ground; my legs were so weak they couldn't support me. We saw the first signs of what we'd read about at home – 4 or 5 men, slave workers with an obvious German in charge, wearing jackboots and lumber jacket, beating two that were lagging behind with a heavy stick across their shoulders. I could feel each blow myself as I watched. So this was the German way and we hadn't believed it at home!

We marched down to a road, we could see a big camp over the other side and the outskirts of a small town up the road. As we approached the main gate to the camp we noticed the high barbed wire fence. A German passed us dressed all in black, smart breaches, swastikas all over him, he must have been one of Himmlers Corps. The gates opened and there was a high sort of monument on the left, an eagle on top – 'Ein Reich, Ein Volk, Ein Fuhrer' – 'We're here now all right!' I murmured.

Two of our Vickers faced us at the gate. We were searched again, then marched down to open ground where we stood for hours. Hungrily, we watched Indian troops making meals. Then we were grouped off in Regiments and our particulars were taken. We were then given more bread and ersatz tea (it was horrible!).

After that we were taken up to some big marquees, five in a row. They were deep in straw, and we were given two mangy blankets and a rusty mess tin. The marquees were already full, so we went over to the two brick buildings opposite – the Americans were in one, mostly in 3-tier bunks. We lay near them on the floor and felt completely lost. A short while later an American NCO told us all to get out in no uncertain terms! So we went into the other one and found a corner up the top of an alley between the bunks. Four of us lay together to keep warm and we forgot about eating food.

The next morning we were paraded for roll call and counted three or four times. Breakfast was ersatz tea and bread, a spoonful of jam and an inch square of butter. We were paraded again and passed through another building where more particulars, trades etc. were taken. I printed a letter card home (we were shown what to write). I was given the number 26090.

I wandered about among the marquees, looking for old faces, asking about pals and found four of our boys, two had been wounded, bullets had been taken out of their legs. They had been patched up, then sent back out with their trousers torn in two – they wanted safety pins to make themselves half-decent again. I talked amongst our boys and speculated when would it finish? 'Maybe November – maybe home for Christmas' was the hope.

Dinner arrived and we lined up in squads for a pint of mangold 'stew', (it was revolting!), but I tried to eat as much as I could. The lavatory was opposite – just two lines of pots, it stank! There was a wire between us and the 'Ruskies' in the next compound. There were guards patrolling on the outside and guards walking around the inside of the wire. Some didn't bother us at all, but others were really

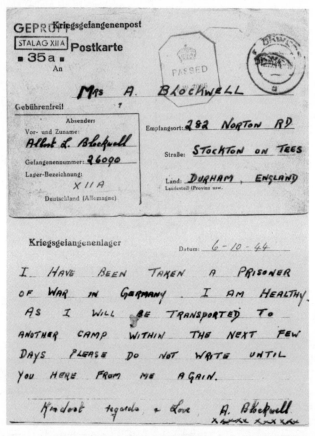

Postkarte from Stalag XIIA. Albert's first letter home from Stalag XIIA on 6th October 1944. All such letters from the camp written by other prisoners were almost identically phrased (Editor's collection)

wicked. No towels, razors or anything were supplied so a wash was out of the question. Someone produced a pack of cards and we played 'Rummy' to pass the time away. The hunger was gnawing at us all the time.

Days passed. We were still unable to find a suitable place to sleep. Two of us lay near the tent opening. The conditions were diabolical – the mud, the filth, no lights, nobody allowed outside after dark (about 6.30 pm) The men started making water all around the opening, including us – the stink was absolutely awful!

After a couple of days we were issued with towels, razors, brushes, etc. – each to be shared between three or four men. The water was turned on ½ hour each morning – about 24 taps for over 2,000 men! I managed a quick wash about every third day. 'How long will we exist in this hole?' we wondered. The Americans were in the end tent – each night, before dark, they held a religious service in the open and I stood in the group and prayed with them.

We were given some horrible, tasteless 'stews' – sometimes bean stalks, sometimes mangolds, sometimes turnip and carrot, all just boiled in water. Then we

No. _cy/REME/2_
(If replying, please quote above No.)

Army Form B. 104—83

_R. E. M. E._ ....Record Office,

2A TICHBORNE ST, ...

LEICESTER. 11 OCT. 1944

SIR ~~OR MADAM~~,

I regret to have to inform you that a report has been received from

the War Office to the effect that (No.)_7622135_ (Rank)....._L/Cpl_......

(Name) _BLOCKWELL._ _Albert Leslie_ ....

(Regiment)_ ROYAL ELECTRICAL MECHANICAL ENGINEERS._ ....

was posted as " missing " on the....._25 September 1944,_ ....

while serving in North West Europe ....

~~The report that he is missing does not necessarily mean that he has~~
been killed, as he may be a prisoner of war or temporarily separated
from his regiment.

Official reports that men are prisoners of war take some time to
reach this country, and if he has been captured by the enemy it is
probable that unofficial news will reach you first. In that case I am to
ask you to forward any postcard or letter received at once to this
Office, and it will be returned to you as soon as possible.

Should any further official information be received it will be at once com-
municated to you.

I am,

Mr. Blockwell,   SIR ~~OR MADAM,~~

282, Norton Rd,   Your obedient Servant,

Stockton-on-Tees.   _Jw Fletcher Capt._
                          for Col.
                          Officer in charge of Records.

IMPORTANT.
Any change of your address should be immediately notified to this Office.

Letter from REME (Editor's collection)

were treated to a spoonful of syrup for tea or break. We were issued with Red Cross
parcels, one to share between three men and we treasured our small portion of
food. Inevitably, stealing broke out, hunger was beginning to tell. I started trading
with the 'Ruskies' for bread.

It was raining constantly, outside was now a quagmire, ankle deep in slimy
mud – imagine what it was like inside! The straw was now flat and filthy. We laid in
pairs, or three or four for warmth. It was pitch dark inside so the only thing to do
was to lie down and stay put – we had to urinate where we lay or endeavour to reach
the flap. We were forced to live like animals.

I palled up with three 'Yanks' and sat and talked to them to pass the days away.
They were interesting chaps, homely – and we talked of our homes, comparing
England with the USA etc. We shared a cigarette four ways. Some big air raids
passed over and we thought it was a hopeful sight. After the 'all clear' one
Messerschmidt flew over – and we all laughed!

A Red Cross official paid us a visit but it was just a farce. When the German NCOs walked round, and sometimes the Officers, we were told to salute them as we did our own – but we resented this. We noticed the German soldiers all saluted their NCOs nazi style, their discipline was obviously very strict.

The weeks dragged by. The lads started with a form of dysentery. They laid amongst us in their dirty pants – well, it can be imagined what it was like – and the smell too!

On the fifth week we moved into a brick building which was a bit cleaner, but still no beds, of course. I noticed a familiar face there but couldn't place it. Batches were moving out now, we wondered when we would move. Another Red Cross issue arrived so I ate chocolate, raisins etc. with great relish but then started with diarrhoea myself! We moved the following day. We marched out of the gates and hoped never to see the place again. They were the five most horrible weeks of my life!

45

Box-cars again!

We were marched into the boxcars once more and found the same crowd was inside. 'How long this time?' we wondered. It was the same as before, far too crowded to lie down comfortably. They were considerate on this occasion however, there was a bin put in for our convenience. I was the first to sit on the bin, I had it good and proper!

Whilst we were talking in the dark, somebody mentioned Stockton. I asked who he was and he said 'Bibby', who had been an old school mate, now I remembered that face. What a strange meeting it was after such a long time.

Another night and day passed, we saw more bombing and travelled through goods yards where there had been total destruction of the rails and wagons, etc. The train halted in sidings for two or three nights – and we all hoped our RAF would stay away. We heard the sound of the sirens for two nights and listened to the drone of the 'planes but they passed over – what a relief! More days and nights passed again. Each morning I hoped and prayed that was the last one, I couldn't see how I could face yet another night.

Another five days and nights were spent in those conditions, the only relief we had was the fact that we would get there someday. We saw an engine in a crater and the damage at Gottingen, we passed Leipzig, saw new lorries, and finally halted in a lonely siding.

The doors opened and we stumbled out, silent, 'Thank God!' we all thought as one.

46

Stalag IVB Muhlberg

We marched off down the road, followed a cart track and passed several farmhouses. We were told to halt in a wood and had another check-up. Then marched down the road again, there was nothing but open countryside for miles.

Suddenly, the prison camp was in sight, with high wire, buildings, and sentry towers at the corners. Thousands of men were close to the wire, watching us arrive. There were only a few Red Berets here and there, many of them had never seen Airborne troops before in any number. We were taken to another part of the camp outside the main enclosure and shown into small marquees. As we marched past a wire enclosure with French or another nationality inside (we couldn't understand their language) we knew they were interested only in our news. We whispered 'Arnhem, Holland / Americanish Cologne'. Their eyes lit up with understanding.

We were given some more bread and some form of spinach stewed up (it was a horrible taste!) but we had to eat anything now to fill our stomachs and if possible to keep a little energy.

Later, we were marched down to the main gate. There was a big wooden archway, with a sentry box on top and searchlight and machine guns poking out. The name 'Stammlager IVB' was over the gate.

We were marched round to the open compound where more particulars were taken, they searched us again, then round to another building and we were

A group of British prisoners en route to Stalag XIIA. Photograph taken at the village of Ellecom, east of Arnhem (Bundesarchiv 590/2330/5)

When the column approaches at least three Borderers are visible: Lance-Corporal
'Smokey Joe' Lothian, C Company clerk (with spectacles ... and cigarette); on his right
Lance-Sergeant Frank Hooper, Signal Platoon and between Lothian and the soldier on
his left is an unidentified Borderer (notice Leslie tartan)
(Bundesarchiv 590/2330/7A)

given two mangy blankets. We then went to another compound where our
clothes were fumigated, we bathed, and then finally we were shown to our
building in the dark, as there was an air raid in progress. We stumbled about inside, groping around, felt 3-tier bunks with half the boards missing and years
old palliasses. I found one unoccupied so I quickly scrambled in and mercifully
huddled down, with all my clothes on except my boots. I felt things crawling
over my feet, legs and neck and thought it must be me that was itchy, but it
went on all night.

At daybreak I got a look around. There was a Sergeant Major in charge. At
7.00 am we were ordered outside into the big compound, all lined up to be counted
and then dismissed. The Sergeant Major gave us the 'gen' and real tea etc. (what a
treat!) Then came 'Skilly up', spuds separate from the pea, mangold and macaroni
'stew'.

Then we all had to vacate for sweep out, so we walked round and round the
compound and buildings – thousands were doing the same thing.

A week passed and we all settled down a bit. My dysentery was getting worse
and I found there were bugs in my bed. I was able to clean up a little and I reported
on sick parade. I was given pills and nothing to eat. After three days I was still no
better and I was finally taken in 'dock'. I felt very weak, I only weighed 57Kilo. (8
st. odd) so I had lost nearly 4 st. since I left Blighty. I was given treatment for 10
days then let out again.

Batches of men had gone out, working 'Kommandos'. We tried to hear the
BBC news – the speculation and rumours were rife, 'Maybe the war would end

about February or March' we all hoped. We heard that there was an American set-back and more prisoners came in which made it even more crowded out.

We started to get organised and had shows in the huts, church services, foot-ball matches, theatre shows, markets, clothes issues – and a wonderful spirit pre-vailed. I felt terribly cold but a bit stronger, however still very thin. I had a helping hand from a Norton chap. All the nationalities were fantastic, there was a great sense of comradeship. We swapped stories, ours sounded feeble compared with the others (they had wicked guards). We heard Warsaw was in uprising. Then civilian prisoners came in with us – women and kids – unbelievable!

We had to be inside at 8.00 pm and there were searchlights all around the camp. The air raid alarms went off most nights and then we were plunged into darkness. The Russians were grovelling around for scraps to eat – they were really starving. The nearby oxen carts gave off a terrible stink, which almost killed any ap-petite we had for the food. I did spud fatigue on the clams.

The gate of Stalag IVB near Muhlberg, one of the largest POW camps
(Rijksmuseum Amsterdam NG-1983-9, Dick van Maarseveen)

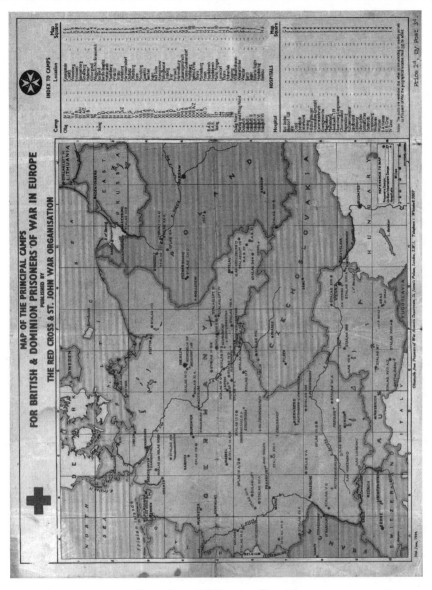

Map of camps (Editor's collection)

47

'Kommando'

It then became my turn for 'Kommando'. About 100 of us marched out down to a small station and pushed into boxcars again, but luckily these were not crowded. When the doors opened we discovered two guards in each car. We talked to them and swapped photographs. After a while we arrived at a small station and we were marched off to the camp, where there were good, warm huts. There was a factory in the distance, about 1mile away. Our manual work started early in the morning, with a pick and shovel, and we were back at 5.30 pm. However our rations were raised to keep up our strength.

There were many air raids and each time we were marched to a shelter under a hill, which was a disused mineshaft. We worked alongside Russians and the French, and some of them stank, they couldn't help it. Then we marched back to camp each night. We were caught outside in one air raid, never again – it was terrifying! The ground we had to dig was hard, the work was useless, heart breaking and meaningless, 'How long was this going to go on?' we wondered.

There was trouble in the camp and two of us sorted it out. We were taken to Gliena 123, Barn building. The Sergeant Major there was a pig, he believed in hard discipline, Gefreiter Schnieder, (who was Bogart in person!), a real tough guy.

Each Sunday we worked on the farm filling in bomb holes. The morale dropped and a lot of stealing broke out in the camp. No letters had been received and we all wondered about home, we didn't hear anything in our camp. There was a lot of speculation on an escape plan. We tried to get news each day from the factory and compared details with others.

When air raids where on while we were in the camp they locked us in. The factory was badly hit but we still had to carry on repairing it, they were stubborn, those Germans! There were many air raids during the day – we spent hours down in the shelters then. One old sentry was pretty good to us when we behaved, but I was once caught pinching turnips and so spent the night in the lock-up!

The Yanks were camped opposite us. Their guards were wicked, we often heard the beatings they were dishing out and ten lads died while we were there. Some of the French Canadians were quite strange but others were O.K. Sometimes we were downstairs during the air raids and we watched with awe at all the lights. In the house opposite, the people were still living in it.

There were no washing facilities provided, so we had an occasional shower down the road. Like others, I began to feel lousy and suffered with scabies. I had no change of clothing and I used some pyjamas for extra warmth – they were really filthy. The cold was intense, I was very thankful for my greatcoat, but my Army boots had worn out after the miles of marching, so I was issued with a pair of clogs (my feet never did get used to them!). The work was very hard, but the cold was even worse.

There were some good jobs outside the factory, there were French guards there. However, there was one OT (Organisation Todt[1]) man who looked and

1   The German civil engineering organisation

acted wicked. I could see big tunnel shelters under a hill filled with thousands of Jews. I watched them every day – they were such a sorry sight, in a horrible state, it seemed to me the Jews that died were the lucky ones – I thought to myself 'The dead had nothing to worry about'. The SS guards were brutal to them.

During some air raids at night we were taken out to the fields, where we could lay and watch our bombers in the searchlights. That was a wicked place – we never had a minute's peace – constant hard labour apart from when the air raids were in progress, and then it wasn't exactly relaxation!

On Saturdays we finished about 2 pm at the factory and brought back spades etc. with us. We were then immediately taken out to fill in the bomb craters in the village and repair the roofs. We didn't even have time to wash. Sundays were the same, sometimes we worked in the factory, if not, we filled in craters in the fields. The Germans were wily, they gave us two craters to fill in, what a job it was! They were big enough to drop a bus into! 'Fill in these and you can go back to camp' they promised. We filled in our two and then were shown another two to fill in – this was a typical German trick! Schnieder would then come on the scene and started bullying and shouting if anyone leaned on a shovel.

Conditions in the camp were wicked, enough to get one down. The stealing among men became worse – even if a slice of bread was laid down, it was stolen. Mate stole from mate, no-one could help it …. satisfying hunger was the top priority. I came back one night and found my small share of the Red Cross parcel had been rifled. Half a dozen men had been around camp that day doing repairs or were sick and we found that some bread and tinned food had been stolen – it was enough to break one's heart. A small portion of bread in the camp was treasured like a wad of banknotes back home.

Early one morning, I dashed out in the dark and crept over to the clams. I stole a couple of handfuls of spuds and risked the punishment. I put the spuds on a wire and dropped them into the stove, the spuds were black and tasted of gas fumes, but I still ate the lot with 'scilly', I would do anything just to fill up. I was still so hungry all the time, so I bought extra bread rations from a lad for cigarettes, three for a ration. It was amazing what men would do for a smoke! The same men were half dying and very skinny.

All the prisoners were becoming very depressed. A mate next to me was interested in motorbikes and racing so we talked for a while, but there was always hunger first, we couldn't get our minds off food. After laying down for an hour or two, I felt very weak when I stood up. My legs were wobbly and I blacked out when I was bending down, I knew I was getting weaker, I wondered 'How long could we carry on?'

No parcels were received for weeks and the rations were scarce. The Irish lad was causing trouble again, he was in charge of distribution and chocolate and cigarettes were missing from stock – of course he blamed the Germans. Schnieder was always smoking, nobody trusted a soul, maybe they traded cigarettes for bread or soup, but we were powerless to do anything.

The Sergeant Major had a sick parade at night, what a farce! He gave out soot pills for dysentery and cut foot blisters and boils with a pocket knife! Sergeant Major came round the beds, there was trouble if a box was found on a bed, he tried to maintain strict discipline as if we were in the German Army. During the roll call mornings and nights, we lined up to get counted. Sergeant Major came out and gave the Nazi salute, I thought, 'I could laugh if I felt like laughing!'

The work in the factory was never finished, there was endless bomb damage and craters to fill in. We started shovelling early in the morning and thought 'Well, another whole day to fill in, a whole day of hard labour in front of us, with nothing to eat and nothing fit to drink!'

All the way to work in the morning I was thinking about breakfast at home, what it would be like when I got back to Blighty, sitting at a table and eating a good meal. Thinking, thinking, all the time I was shovelling ... what would I like to do when I got home, maybe visit some shops, a snack bar ... back to food again – it was so horrible to be hungry. I talked to a chap as we worked, he had been a servant and talked of cooking for the gentry etc. He was very interesting to talk to, he described all the wonderful dishes they had, until the lads told us to stop it.

I made friends with a decent chap, an 'Aussie'. At first he said he was caught in Italy. Later he said he was a Warrant Officer in the RAF. He was the only decent bloke I had come across, he had never lost his pride and I could trust him. I shared a cigarette with him, me a draw, him a draw, then nip.

There was constant trouble amongst the men, a few were always around the fire – we were all supposed to take turns at getting a warm, they were arguing constantly.

The work was absolutely meaningless. We started filling in the craters, and then taken to another place and started digging a trench for drains, then taken back to the craters again. We hoped and prayed for sirens, which gave us a break, perhaps an hour or two in a shelter, or better still, across the fields. The shelters were cold, dark and inhospitable.

Digging the drains one day, the 'Aussie' laid down his shovel and said he was going for 'the usual' in the crater – there was no guard in sight. The 'Aussie' did not come back. We were counted up before we went back and he was found missing – what trouble that caused! The Sergeant Major went frantic, he stopped the cigarette issue and cut the food ration down. Two men above me, old soldier types, had a map and they were always talking of escape between themselves.

Another raid began one night, the sirens sounded, it seemed bright with flares all round – when we looked out of the windows we could see the flares were all round us, it was to be right on the factory! We heard the droning coming nearer and nearer, right over us. We crouched on our beds, locked in, unable to escape our fate. The first bombs crashed down and the building shook. There was a terrible thunder of engines, drowned by the crashing thunder of the bombs. One long, crashing thunder without a pause. I lit up a cigarette, pulled hard, a hundred thoughts went through my mind. I said to myself 'This is perhaps my last fag!' I was shaking a little, heart pumping, there was a big crash right outside and all the windows were blown out. The slates came off the roof, then after about 20 minutes the engines faded off. All was quiet and we breathed again.

In the morning we went out to see the damage. There was a crater about 12 feet from the end of our building, the bomb had landed on the spud clams – the soft ground had deadened the blast. Anywhere else and our building would have come down and I would not have lived to tell the tale. The guard huts were covered with earth, our hearts sank, if only it had landed about 20 feet the other way!

The wire was all down and a party was detailed to repair the wire. An American in a coffin had been blown up, his body lay a little way off. We had no lights and no water now. We went down to a small village a kilometre away and it was wiped out – not a house left whole. There was earth and bricks everywhere. It was impossible to make any impression on the mess even if we worked for six months.

On Sunday we were taken to a farmhouse across the road to help with carrying slates. The cemetery was blown to pieces, with craters in every direction. I thought 'The Germans are such stubborn people, they will never give up!' When we were marching back to the factory, we could see it in the distance, it was a mess – and still smoking. The roads were impassable, so we started filling in craters. We thought and hoped 'Surely they'll give up now?' 'Maybe we'll go back to Stalag IVB.'

The fields opposite were covered with holes – dozens ... scores.

Day after day our task was clearing the damage, filling in craters, with not a hope of them giving in. A couple of days later, windows were re-fitted in the main offices and also stoves – what a stubborn race!

We were taken over the fields at the weekend, the craters covered the fields. We started filling them in, what a hopeless task it was, 1,000 men were needed to make any impression whatsoever. We could see the road from the fields where we were working. Dozens of refugees were trudging along the road, and the German Army with horse-drawn carts heading towards Zeity, away from Dresden, maybe. There were also Army vehicles, with OT guards on the mudguards, which we took as a good sign our front was near. We heard sirens and could see Fighters in the distance. There was hope in our hearts.

We came back from the factory along the railway and every wagon was damaged. The workers' train came in every morning, terribly crowded, compared with trains back home. Sirens went off and everybody was really scared and they all scattered. The road was filled with workers – Russians and Jews, and the Germans, all batting up the road towards the shelters as fast as they could run, anywhere away from the factory.

Schnieder was a queer man, he had a hatred for desk soldiers. There were many arguments at the shelters, he told the Army Officers and civilians to get out to let us in. He had his name taken many a time. Once, the guard stopped our men carrying something for him so he had another argument with them. Schnieder cared for no-one, he was a soldier true bred, hard on discipline and hated anybody who had not been at the front, such as OT men or works police, etc.

We often saw the Yanks beaten, they seemed to have wicked guards.

The Jews were in a terrible state, we watched them trudge past and watched the SS guards beat them for no reason. One day one lay near us, as near dead as possible, but we were not allowed to touch him. He lay there all day – and died, I guess. Often going back at night we would hear a shot and see Jews carrying another Jew – 'What was life?' I asked myself.

The OT guards were taken away and civvy guards took over. We surmised our front must have been getting closer. A funny old chap looked after us who reminded me of Charlie Chaplin. He was just an ordinary old chap, quite decent and he traded bread for us.

Meanwhile, two of our lads had escaped out of a hole in the roof made by bombs, they got away O.K. – we were not surprised. The Germans were frantic again because of the escape and they blamed the Yanks for letting them go out with them.

Some days we would go across the fields away from the factory, digging banks of drains etc. We were pleased to be away from the factory. Sirens went off and we laid in dykes and watched to see if Forts & Libs were going over. 'Would this go on much longer?' I thought.

It was the most senseless work in the factory. Everywhere was chaos – a mass of craters, rubble, pipes, damage everywhere and plants destroyed. The Powerhouse had been blown up and the clock had stopped on the wall at 10.12 pm.

Another day raid occurred whilst we were working outside on the drainage. Forts came over, nearer and nearer and we all scattered over the fields, getting as far away from the factory as possible. We laid in a gully and the formation flew right over us. The bombs came swishing, whistling down, the ground trembled (so did we!) and the bombs burst all around us. I breathed again. Another formation came and the same thing happened again.

When we went back to the factory there was another mess waiting for us to clear up. 'How much more of this?' I wondered. There were hundreds of unexploded bombs in the area – hundreds! They were some of our 4,000 pounders. The Jews were made to drag the bombs about all day, clearing them away. Alas, there were more bombs round the factory than were on it – what a pity!

When we watched the Forts going away, we thought of them going home. They would be home in a few hours – how wishful and envious we felt. Flare canisters were laid about with English words written on them, it brought back a bit of home just to see them. Silver paper was laid all over after a night raid and leaflets were scattered all over the countryside. Going to work after a night raid, there were leaflets everywhere, fields, roofs, roads – millions of them. Somebody tried to pick one up and Schnieder shouted. I picked one up quickly and stuffed it inside my coat.

The days and the weeks dragged on, with new rumours every day. All the OT guards had now gone and the civvy guards had completely taken over. One or two of them were a bit talkative. We inquired from them when they were on their own. 'Ruskies 50 Km from Berlin!' they whispered. We understood. They glanced around when they spoke to us as they were obviously scared of the Gestapo. The French workers were always a source of 'gen'. When any were near us we asked them for news. 'Our Army is getting closer – Weimar!' There was news of a big airborne landing, thousands of paratroopers, they said.

We were always on the scout for food. Anybody who looked 'friendly' we asked for 'bread'. If they had any, we pushed our luck and said '15 cigarettes?' I felt very weak, hardly slept at all because I itched all night, – I started with scabies.

April began and we said 'Maybe this will be the last month!' We were all taken to Zeity to a sort of barracks for X-rays. In the camp we got a visit from a civvy who spoke English. We read between the lines, things were getting very close!

48

The Exodus

On Thursday, 12th April we went to the factory as usual. 8 or 10 of us were across the field working on a bank of drains. The sirens sounded and the guard made for a gully. The fighters were in the distance and the bombers were near us, the bombs dropped a few miles away all around us. About noon, Schnieder came along and we shouted for the guard. They talked a bit then marched us back to the factory. Schnieder seemed very quiet and we wondered, 'What is it? Have they given up?'

When we went into the factory all the workers seemed to be leaving. We met some of our other lads who said our tanks were about 5 miles away! We still didn't believe it, we couldn't!

On the way back, fighters went overhead – Typhoons. Now we knew they were so close, it was good to see them. We all felt cheerful, 'Hope is wonderful!'

Back at the camp, we wondered what was to happen. We noticed the guards had taken off their revolvers. I made my bread into a sandwich and made up my mind. 'If we go out tonight, I'm going to beat it!' I promised myself.

During the night there was heavy shellfire close by. 88 mm fire a few miles off and mortars. In the early morning we could hear machine gun fire – our machine guns! We all became very excited as dawn was breaking. We stood by the window watching, waiting, hoping – and praying! We could hear firing in the distance. Then the Sgt. Major gave us some good soup for breakfast.

About 20 of us were assembled in the yard, the sick stayed behind. We were all marched out, up the road towards Altenburgh. We trudged along mile after mile, all strung out. When fighters came over, we lay in the roadside, praying they wouldn't see us. We rested a while and the guards talked to the civvies. There was a lot of confusion, the civvies pointed one way and the guards another, I don't think they knew where to go. We went down a side road towards a village. One or two German lorries passed us. We could hear the firing from high ground. 'How long will this be?' we wondered. Mile after mile we marched, then halted in a small town. Our fighters came over again.

On we marched again, down an open road – we could see another road in the distance, with more prisoners on the move. Fighters came over yet again, 'Now we've had it!' I thought. We stopped at the side of the road and took cover the best we could, we felt very exposed. The 'planes had American signs and passed over low, but didn't fire at us. I breathed again.

It was now dark and we were still trudging on. We came to an ex-camp building, which was deserted, so we rested awhile. They told us we had to go on to Altenburgh, about 8 miles. My legs were wobbly and I felt very groggy, I could hardly keep my eyes open. We could see flashes of guns on the high ground, firing at our lads.

We started marching again, mile after mile, then we were halted at a bridge and the guards talked together. They told us to walk in single file over it, the bridge was apparently mined. We said a little prayer, crossed our fingers, then on again, safe once more, for a while. We passed a hutted camp, and men and women on the roadside, Estonians or Russians or something. We eventually reached a big barracks and a prisoner camp, Stalag IVF[1]. It was all deserted, so we squatted down where we were and fought to keep our eyes open, in a sort of daze. We thought we might be allowed to rest there for the night but in an hour or so we were marched off again. 'I can't go on much further!' I thought. I talked to a Scottish lad and told him I was going to drop out at the first chance I got, and he said he was game.

1   Stalag IVF was located at Hartsmandorf Chemnitz

49

The Escape

It was a pitch-dark night and after walking for a seemingly endless time we reached that same camp again! – We must have walked in a circle! The Germans were totally confused, so we stopped for a few minutes and I said to my mate 'Come on, this is our chance!' We made off towards some huts up a path and two other lads followed us, all creeping as quietly as possible. When we were well away from the road we crouched by the huts and expected the guards to come shouting after us. We heard the guards shouting, but then heard our lads start moving off again, and after a few minutes the noise faded.

We could hardly believe that we were on our own at last. We listened by the windows of a hut, but we couldn't hear a sound, we expected to hear screams any second. We moved round to the door, opened it quietly, listened again, it was empty. We groped around in the dark and found a table. We lay down by the wall, under the table as protected as we could, and huddled together to keep warm. I slept soundly, I was so exhausted, but was rudely wakened by someone trying to drag my coat off me. I rose quickly – it was a German civvy on the scrounge.

I got up, the camp was deserted apart from a few civvies carting away furniture. I asked for food and the civvy made like he understood. I gave him a helping hand with a vice, which he was taking and he gave me food as repayment. I reversed my red beret, and Jock said 'Mind he doesn't give you away'. I hesitated, thought about it, and then chanced it. We walked out of the camp onto a road and a few German troops were coming towards us – Luftwaffe NCOs! I thought 'Too late now!' I held my breath, 'Don't look at me!' I glanced at them casually and passed them.

I had a sandwich, which I managed to make in a nearby house then I returned to the camp. During the morning firing broke out close by. We saw German troops coming back across the fields, running along the hedgerow, firing occasionally and we heard our lads firing back. We wondered what would happen if the Germans came into this camp – it would be a target for our own mortars!

Jock came back in from a scrounge and said he had found some Yank prisoners in another hut, so we went over to them. I opened the door and saw jackboots and grey uniform legs! My heart gave a leap. I stopped, hesitated, then a Yank said 'Come on in'. I pushed open the door and found two more of our lads and two Yanks. I said 'Who is this?' and he said 'A Russian'. We lay around all day and heard lorries on the road and saw loads of troops going away from the town.

During the afternoon some Germans came into the camp and a kid ran over and told them about us. We watched and they looked as if they were giving up, tearing off their armbands. Some came over to our hut – 'This is it!' we thought. We waited for them to come in. They asked us something in German, which we didn't understand. I said 'Gefangeners'. They said something about 'Posten' and we shrugged our shoulders. They looked around and went out.

Another night passed. The next morning the Fighters were patrolling. We could see a convoy on a road in the distance but it was too far to see what they were. One or two seemed to be in front on recce. 'They must be ours!' we thought, but didn't feel inclined to put our feelings to the test. An aerodrome was also over in the distance. Two Serbs went into town and they came back later. They said there were American tanks in town! We couldn't believe it, we just couldn't believe it was all over.

Suddenly, there was a noise down the road and Jeeps went by. We rushed out onto the roadside. Lorries, tanks and American troops, were all driving passed! We became very emotional and threw them kisses, they threw back cigarettes to us. I went down the road a short way and found Infantry on the roadside. We talked a bit and they piled me up with food. I went back to the hut with the first food for three days – the first real food for months! I said 'Today we eat!'

Then we gathered our belongings and made for town. We exchanged greetings with Yank drivers. The town was deserted with only a few civvies here and there. I was loaded up with cigarettes. The ex-Stalag was full of French and we went in and talked a bit. I found a storeroom and dug up a pair of old boots to fit and threw my clogs away – heaven! We found a big house that was empty and made ourselves at home. We made supper, smoked and made plans for the morning. 'We were free!' We still couldn't believe it!

In the morning we went down to a garage and broke open the door. We found a good car and I got it going. We got some petrol from the Yanks and asked which way to go back. We started off, on top of the world, driving along, smoking, with plenty of chocolate, biscuits and cheese on the seat. We drove along the road we had trudged along. We passed by the old camp at Gliena – what memories now! I had an urge to go and find Schnieder and the Sgt. Major ... but I didn't have a gun!

We passed on and asked an MP in Zeity for the road back. After following directions we went onto an Autobahn and the road was deserted. It was a lonely feeling with no Yank lorries in sight. We were rather worried, 'Suppose we were on the wrong road and run into Germans?' We stopped at a house and the people talked, gushing to tell us 'Estonians'. They made us coffee and we gave the kids chocolate and oranges. Then on we went again.

We motored on along this main road feeling very lonely – there was nothing else in sight. We expected to find convoys of lorries, tanks and troops, but we realised that Battle Groups were covering the country, just covering ground and taking on any Germans they found. We still had that feeling of running into trouble – we thought it best not to carry any guns. If we ran into German troops we might get away by saying we were ex-prisoners, unless they were S.S., but our luck held out.

We came across some American MPs and they were a bit suspicious of us. We showed our number tags and gave them a good drink of a bottle we had been given. Then we told them to keep the bottle when they said they were to clear any traffic off the main roads, ready for Army traffic. They told us to get moving quickly.

We started to see columns of people – old folk, women, and kids, mostly in poor clothes, rags and the striped clothes of the concentration camps. They were all trudging along or riding on horse and carts. Some had a French flag on their cart – all were going one way .... away from Germany ... all going west.

The sight of those people choked us a bit – they were the real refugees – it wasn't a film – most only had what they stood up in. Most had left their families in the concentration camps. They had to keep to the fields, off the roads.

They all looked dirty, but I don't suppose they minded that, we were just as dirty, we had lost the habit of washing long ago! The worst part of the hell-holes we finished in was being deprived of everything we took for granted – no washing water – no shaving – no toilet. Only a dustbin to sit on in the barrack block and this was often overflowing on the floor.

The blankets we had and the bunks were infested with bugs, lice, etc. As soon as we lay down they moved over our legs and faces – but the constant aching in our stomachs for some food was the worst – we were getting thinner all the time. Getting up in the morning – no breakfast – going off to the factory – all day to face and nothing to eat – and the freezing cold.

When I looked at those refugees I knew just how they felt – but now they were going home. We were all going to go home! After a few more miles, the car conked out! A young woman was standing by a farm gate so we pointed to the car and made out we wanted bed and food. She got a horse and pulled us into the farmyard. A Black American was in the yard, he said his truck had broken down. We went into the house and found 5 or 6 people in there, men and women, who gave us some eggs. Later 3 or 4 more Blacks came into the house and asked us who we were, then finally went out.

We later heard screaming from the yard, a girl ran into our house and said the Blacks were next door frightening them. I went with her – I didn't feel good (I had no gun), but I bluffed them into leaving the women alone.

Later, we heard further screams – they had come back for the mother. We rushed for the bedroom window but couldn't see a thing. Then we heard 4 shots and their truck pulled out. I went down to the yard with a young woman but I couldn't see anything, so I came back to the house. I thought we should have another search, so we had a good look around – then I found the mother laid out dead. I had to go back to the house and tell them – what a terrible job! Then, we had to decide what to do with the mother. I thought it best to leave her for the MPs in the morning. I felt awful, her laid out there all night. They gave us a bedroom, but we couldn't sleep, we were listening out for truck noises most of the night. In the morning we were glad to get out. I felt rotten about the mother and when the MPs came along we stopped them and told the whole story.

They gave us a lift to a small town called Bad Sulsa where we saw an officer who wrote out a statement. He asked if we could identify them, but we said we were not sure, it was dark. We didn't want to be held up for any court case – and the thought of going along trying to pick them out in a line-up put us off – after all, life still seemed cheap to us. All those killed in bomber raids and the camps – GIs being killed every day as we talked – what was one woman? There was something rotten about sheer murder though.

We were taken on to the next town near Gotha – ex-Army barracks, all full of British, French, Poles, all PoWs. I managed to clean up a bit and watched some German girls with GIs cavorting about over on the hillside. If only the Germans, who were still fighting a few miles away, knew about that!

Next we moved to a Schloss (castle) on the top of a hill. We lay on the floor in big, empty rooms and cans of fruit, rice, milk, etc. were handed around – I had to find someone with a tin opener! Mostly we just drank from tins – since our capture we had no issue of forks, spoons, etc. I only had a knife, which I had traded for 3

To Lieut.-Colonel R. D. Sellon and All Ranks of the 7th (Galloway) Battalion The King's Own Scottish Borderers.

ORDER OF THE DAY
By
Brigadier R. H. BOWER, C.B.E., Comd. 1st Air Landing Brigade.

In November 1943 your Battalion was ordered to assume an airborne role and join the 1st Air Landing Brigade.

As soon as this became generally known the greatest enthusiasm was displayed by all ranks and it became a matter of difficulty to meet your urgent demands for gliders and for airborne training.

That spirit persisted, and animating all ranks finally found its full outlet in the magnificent action fought by the Battalion at Arnhem in September, 1944.

Returning from Holland the ranks of the Battalion were depleted and it was not until 1st January, 1945, that reinforcements arrived.

It then became a matter of great urgency to reform the Battalion which was to be ready to take part in operations in May. Although Officers, N.C.O.'s, and men came from many different Units everybody worked with a single object and with the greatest enthusiasm and cheerfulness.

Due to the ending of the war in Europe no further fighting was necessary but the subsequent work of the Battalion in Norway earned it high praise.

The Battalion having now finished its airborne duties with great credit can feel that it has added a worthy chapter to the history of The King's Own Scottish Borderers.

I sincerely thank you for your hard work and for your cheerful co-operation and I wish you the best of luck in the future wherever you may be.

22nd October, 1945.

R. H. BOWER, *Brigadier.*

Order of the Day
(Courtesy Robert Sigmond)

cigarettes from a Russian. Someone started up a large square stove in the corridor so I thought I'd have some rice pudding. I opened the tin and put it on the stove. After a while it started bubbling over, more and more. We tried to keep pace with the rice, but we never did!

Shortly after we were told to move. We still seemed to be in a bit of a daze – I don't remember anyone talking much. We were all suffering from the effects of lack of food, hunger, weakness and filth over the past 7 months, and still didn't really believe it was all over.

Someone said we were going to the airfield – it was unbelievable! We got to the field and saw dozens of Dakotas lined up. We boarded and took off, hoping we would not be shot down – it was still possible – but after an hour or so we felt safe.

There was a shout – 'The White Cliffs!' – we circled round, down and landed. Someone said – 'Le Havre' – so we were a bit disappointed. We were stripped off and white powder was sprayed all over us. Then we were taken to tents with stoves in the centre – they were warm and dry. There were bunks for four in a tent with blankets. A loudspeaker was playing 'Don't fence me in' – it was slowly coming to us, we were back to normal!

Then we were moved down to the docks and boarded a ship. After dark we moved out and the doors were locked, which made us realise the war was still on and we were still in danger.

50

Back to Blighty

The morning brought us into Southampton with a band playing on the dock-side in our honour. Then we were off in the lines of lorries waiting for us, and away to a camp nearby.

The loudspeaker called out 'NAAFI open' and we went over and lined up for tea. The girl said '2d.' and we looked at her in amazement! I said 'I've just come from a PoW camp' but that made no difference – it was still '2d.' Someone in the queue kindly paid for me … we were certainly back home!

We were told to line up to make telephone calls – we were allowed one call home. I telephoned the shop near my Mother's – what a surprise they must have got!

Someone took all my particulars, name, regiment, etc. My mind flashed back to the last one to ask our particulars – we were told we only had to give name and number, like in the films. The first thing the Germans did was to give us all Red Cross postcards. On a blackboard were a few lines to copy, saying we were alright. Later a German questioned us singly – first he said 'Name, number, home address?' I looked at him and I said I only had to give my name and number … and held my breath! He said it didn't matter, he had it on my postcard! … I felt a bit stupid!

The next day we were on the way home. I give credit to the organisation that got us all moving so quickly. I was home the next morning. It took a good while to settle down – I constantly had the feeling that the meals would not last and that to-morrow there would be nothing left to eat. In addition to that I could not eat a good meal, my stomach had shrunk so much it would only take small meals. My legs also swelled up badly for a long time.

Back from Germany. Albert, 1945
(Editor's collection)

51

Duty calls

I enjoyed 56 days recuperation in the form of leave, then was informed I had to report to Croydon. We started doing rifle training, learning about the PIAT etc. – what a farce! We had to go round an assault course. We had pictures and shows to visit in Croydon so I enjoyed the evenings. However, we felt it was all a waste of time – we were no longer interested in what we were doing.

The next move was to Scorton Workshops (this was near home so I could visit every weekend). Some German prisoners were now working for us on repairing lorries etc. The hard times were soon forgotten (I bought an extra cake for my German each day) – we were almost normal again. The time was spent pleasant enough – I was home every weekend, but the work seemed a complete waste. We were not getting prepared for anything – nothing to train for anymore.

After a few months waiting for demob – my Group finally came up. It was the end of an experience that money couldn't buy – which turned out lucky for me.

Release leave certificate
(Editor's collection)

Army Form X 202B.

67364

CERTIFICATE OF TRANSFER to the ARMY RESERVE

Army No. ...76.221.35......   Rank .......C.F.N........

Surname (Block letters)............BLOCKWELL.............

Christian Name(s) ....ALBERT. LESLIE,.........

Regt. or Corps ......R.E.M.E.................................

The transfer of the above-named to the appropriate Class of the Army

Reserve (see note below) is confirmed with effect from ......5 . 7 . 46 .

*The date to be inserted here will be that following the day on which Release Leave terminates, including any additional leave to which the soldier may be entitled by virtue of service overseas.

Note.—The appropriate Class of the Army Reserve is as follows:—

(i) Royal Army Reserve—in the case of a regular soldier with reserve service to complete:

(ii) Army Reserve Class Z (T)—in the case of a man of the Territorial Army, including those called up for service under the National Service Acts:

(iii) Army Reserve, Class Z—in the case of all other soldiers not included in (i) or (ii) above.

Record Office Stamp.

R.E.M.E. RECORDS

LEICESTER

....

Officer i/c ..R.E.M.E....... Records.

Date .9.-5.-46...........

Warning.—

Any alteration of the particulars given in this certificate may render the holder liable to prosecution under the Seamen's and Soldiers' False Characters Act, 1906.

If this certificate is lost or mislaid, no duplicate can be obtained.

Wt. 37285/90 1,000M 12/45 KJL/1516/16 Gp. 38/3

Certificate of transfer
(Editor's collection)

52

Counting my blessings

So, briefly, those are the chapters of my life in the Army up to the time I went into action against the Germans, subsequently captured, a Prisoner of War and eventually my return to England.

I look back to those first war months and my first months in the Army. At first it was a fairly good life, new and novel and we were all young together and had a fairly good time.

Not one of us knew what was to come in a few years time, none of us guessed that the war was to go on for years and years – six years of war. Most of us didn't think we would even see action or battlefields. I don't think any of us gave the war a minutes thought. We always had that feeling that 'someone else' would do the fighting – 'someone else' would do the dying. No one thought of being killed personally. As I said before, we were young and light-hearted and didn't give the war more than ordinary interest, wondering how long it would last – would we go to France? Thinking what a good time we would have seeing French towns and cities – how different it was all to be – yes! How different!

As the months rolled on into years we began to get sort of hardened to a new life, had a new outlook on the future. The war wasn't going well for us, every month, every week brought new setbacks for us. We trained hard for many months, learning about new weapons, new tactics, watching the progress of the German armies through the Continent. A new threat now, the Germans were advancing towards Alexandria and Suez, across the North African desert. The Japs were also on the advance towards India. To look at a map of the world it looked like two big pincers or claws trying to close together somewhere about the Suez.

We could realise that the war was to last for many years, in fact, as the years dragged on, we seemed to forget about getting back into Civvy Street. We just sort of resigned ourselves to spend many years in the Army, but for all the gloom the majority of us never thought for a minute that we would lose the war. I, personally, always had a kind of confidence that somehow we would begin to drive the Germans back and win in the end. Although when I looked at our position and when we had our little discussions and arguments by the billet fire, I couldn't see how we were going to beat the Germans. As I often pointed out, look what is against us – it will take us years to drive them back out of Africa and then we have to start on the Continent. Drive them out of the Balkan countries, Italy and finally France. Then in the north we would have to start on Norway and then over the other side there was the Japanese army to drive out of the countries and jungles between India and China. Yes! It was a grim picture to look at and as I say, I for one couldn't possibly see how we were to do all this inside at least six years from then.

Well, one year passed into the next. We in the Infantry units trained over and over again. We had our good times with the bad, but as I often thought, we were lucky to be in England. Even at the worst we were far better off than the boys in the desert or Far East. Although we were prepared to go abroad at any time, it wouldn't have surprised any of us had we got our 'marching orders'.

There were many times when I thought I had been unlucky to be with an Infantry unit – but then again, I often thought that I might have been sent abroad long ago had I been posted to some other unit.

Then there was the time when our Battalion was moved out of the 15th Scottish Division and sent up to the Shetland Islands. We thought we were getting a raw deal again, but as it later turned out we were perhaps lucky. At least, I was, for that Division took part in many of the big battles after the Invasion of France, and maybe I would have not been so lucky as to get through alright.

Then came our next move, into the 1st Airborne Division. Well, once again I thought we were to get the 'sticky end', but as it turned out I was lucky to get through and in the bargain I had the best time of all in that Division. During the months we spent training in the Airborne we had many good times, we travelled up and down the country, had numerous leaves, and had many privileges. Although not without strict discipline – but taking the good with the bad, as before, we had some good times and fun, in those days. Also, we had the added thrills of flying and learning the new tactics of Glider-borne Infantry. To most of us this flying was a thrill, but for me it was a dread. Not the actual flying, for I got the same thrill out of it as most of the other boys did, but as I said before, my stomach wasn't built for flying or ships. Each time I flew, I was feeling sick almost as soon as the wheels left the ground, and as for being scared – I was just as scared as the next man. In fact, I was more scared than most of them, but for all that I had that queer feeling of always wanting to go up and fly again, each time I came down. It was like a 'flying bug' that got into us.

Well, once more it seemed like I was unlucky again, for I was the only Fitter to fly – the other Fitters went over with the Seaborne party. Well, maybe I was unlucky in a way, for the other boys had a good reception in France and Belgium and also later in Norway. However, as everything turned out I was lucky enough to get back, even though I had to suffer months of existing like an animal, suffering mental and physical hardships.

These chapters have given a brief account of the places I visited during my Army life, but of course there were a thousand small things that happened from day to day that I haven't mentioned. For instance, the various conditions we constantly had to live under, the bad food at times, the terrible boredom of living in camps away in the country. All those small things that make Army life monotonous and dreary. Most of those monotonous routines of parades and regulations are the main reason for the dreariness of Army life. Having to parade for every little thing, usually in our own time, the routine of making up beds each day, laying kit out, being put 'on a charge' for small details, such as a little dust, studs missing in boots, blankets not in line as they should have been. A hundred and one things that just made Army life a continuous routine of monotony, that gradually made us fed up with taking orders, doing this or that just as someone else wanted, never being allowed to do anything just as we wanted to do.

It was those small things that made us 'fed up' with Army life – the hard living and rough training we took as a matter of course. We knew we had to train and train hard and so we did our training usually with good heart and took the bad with the good. During most of the hard training we made the best of everything and often had many laughs. Times when we had to lay out in the cold, winter nights, wet and freezing – but as I said before, we took all those hardships as everyday life. We knew we had to learn and perfect our training if ever we were to beat the Germans and get back home. However, as I said, it was the other little irksome duties and regulations that 'browned us off' more than all the training ever did.

There were many times when I got terribly 'fed up' with life in the Army, for instance, during the time I was in the Orkney Isles. I was so 'fed up' of being 'messed about' from day to day by men like the 'Mad Major' that I tried many times to get away from the Battalion. The only way I could think of was to apply for a Sgt. Fitters course. If I passed this course I would have been posted to another unit and very likely posted overseas. Well, if I had got that course (which I didn't) I would probably have gone overseas with some other unit and maybe I wouldn't have been so lucky to get through as I did. So thinking of these things, maybe it was all for the best.

Then finally came the invasion of the Continent – D-Day – and we were in the 1st British Airborne Division. During the months previous to D-Day we thought that we were pretty certain to be in the fore, but as the time drew close we heard talk that the 6th Airborne Division were 'down south' and ready for the big show. Once more we rated ourselves as being lucky, for it seemed like we were not to be 'in it' just yet.

During the months following the invasion we were lucky many times. The first time was when our Army was held up at Caen. We were to drop behind the town and take the Germans in the rear. It was cancelled at the last moment and the following morning we heard that a few Panzer Divisions had moved into that very area – were we lucky!

That made us think about careless talk. It seemed to me many times that too many people knew of our movements. All through the war it was a well-known fact that if we wanted to know about any future move – ask the civvies round about. In my opinion, the biggest leakage of information came, not from the men, but from Officers talking to women and telling their wives. All this censorship was tightened up considerably after D-Day, but around the camps there were still too many NCO's who often 'knew something'. For instance, before we were briefed for one operation, one of our sergeants came in and started talking of what he knew, and finally he hinted at the place we were to drop. Up to then no-one was supposed to know – I didn't like to hear of such information being talked about, for if our men could get it, so could Jerry.

Finally came Arnhem. I didn't like this operation from the start, our men didn't seem to know enough. We asked many questions before we went over, but our Officers couldn't tell us much at all. It seemed to me like it was a rush job and I didn't like it. Well, as I've already written, we dropped at Arnhem and it seemed like the Germans were ready for us. It is my opinion that our Leaders blundered on that operation in many ways.

In the first place our Division should never have been dropped spread out as we were, for by doing that we were already 'cut up' into smaller fighting units, just as Jerry wanted.

In the second place, we shouldn't have dropped beyond our own Artillery support, for as it turned out, we had no heavy guns with which to stop his tanks. Once we had lost our 17 and 6 pounders, we could do nothing but withdraw and defend the best way we could.

Thirdly, it seemed to me like he (Jerry) knew of our moves and intentions many times. The morning we were due to land, at 10.30 am, German Fighters were patrolling the area, shooting up good and proper. Lucky for us we were late owing to fog in Blighty. The following day at 10.30 am the Polish were due to land. Those Fighters again showed up and were shooting everything they could see. Lucky for them, they were late in too. Then, wherever we moved in that area he seemed to be ready for us – no sooner did we dig-in than he would start bombing and shelling us. No! Either Jerry got to know too much, or else he was lucky in anticipating our moves.

Well, I myself, was lucky at Arnhem, for I came through O.K., even though I did do a term in a prison camp, but many were not so lucky. As I looked back I realised how lucky I had been. In the first place I wasn't hit at all, and then the night we made a break, we were all very lucky that we happened to pass along one side of a house when Jerry was at the other side and we didn't know. During the night it was touch or go whether we tried for the river or not. If we had done, I would have probably been killed on the river bank as many others were. Then in the following morning I was all for having another try at making for the river, not knowing that Jerry had us all covered all the time – once again I was still lucky.

Yes, now that I look back on those things I realise I was lucky many times, my luck never seemed to leave me – or maybe I was just destined to come through and come safe home.

Arnhem Bridge after the battle, as seen from the German Mark III Panzer of Karl-Heinz Kracht. On either side lies the debris of wrecked vehicles, lined up to clear a path through to the south.
(Copyright: Kabel-Kracht)

British prisoners under guard in the Eusebius Church

Now, years after, I think back to those days at Arnhem, and I think not of my-self but of all those boys I lived with, slept with, trained with in the years before in Blighty. They were good boys, some bad of course, but then with so many men there were sure to be a few 'bad apples in the barrel'.

When I think of Arnhem, it doesn't signify a town or city to me. The picture I have of Arnhem is a picture of a small wood with small foxholes here and there. Air-borne helmets showing above them, one or two of our boys crouching behind trees, as if licking their wounds.

Another picture is in the dead of night, the broken houses around us are lit up with fire. The constant 'snap' of a sniper's rifle, a few dark-faced figures passing up the street, calling a quiet password.

Another picture is that of us sitting low in our trenches, looking up to the sky at our supply planes dropping our supplies by parachute. Bombers on fire, blazing, but still dropping supplies to us on the ground. As I watch the bravery of those men up there I raised my hand to my helmet in salute.

One more picture is that of us making a final stand in a battered house, outside it is raining hard and as I look out of the window I can see one of our boys laid face down, where he fell, the rain beating down on him, soaking him through. I thought of his people back home – his wife – I felt a little 'nip' in my throat.

Such was Arnhem – and now today, who remembers? Many people today ask, what does that mean? Where was it? When somebody says that I feel like – well, how could I feel? How are they to know anyway, only us who were there really know what Arnhem means and what it stands for.

Was it all worthwhile? Well, I suppose it was war, and in war mistakes are made and somebody gets killed. So there it was, a glorious mistake, but for the men

In May 1978 the Airborne Museum 'Hartenstein' was officially opened by Major-General Urquhart. It had previously been housed at Doorwerth Castle since 1949. The photograph was taken one week before the opening. Opposite the Museum the Airborne Monument, unveiled by Queen Wilhelmina in 1946. This oblique photograph shows the battle area of the 7th Battalion.

1   The Airborne Museum 'Hartenstein'
2   Airborne Monument
3   Utrechtseweg
4   Landing Zone L
5   Railway Ede-Arnhem
6   Johannahoeve farm
7   Deelen airfield
8   The White House
9   Post war buildings
10 Oranjeweg
11 Hartenweg
12 Bothaweg
13 Paul Krugerstraat
14 Nassaulaan
15 Steijnweg
16 Cronjéweg
17 Karel van Gelderlaan

(Courtesy Robert Sigmond)

A same oblique photograph was taken to the south-east showing the Hartenstein
Museum in the foreground again
(Courtesy Robert Sigmond)

who were killed, there is nothing to bring them back. I'm not sorry now that I was
there. No! I am proud. I am proud to say that I was once in the 1st Airborne Division, and I will be forever proud to say that I was with those men that week at
Arnhem. Yes! I'm proud to say today that I was there with those men, and their
memory will stay with me for all time – the memory of all those brave boys and the
way they died.

We were 10,095 strong, fit and lighthearted, full of fight – in one week, or
rather 10 days and nights, we had suffered over 7,500 casualties. In my battalion of
nearly 900 men, 71 men and 4 Officers came back – yes! I was lucky.

I don't believe in ghosts myself, but if there are such things, I know that the
ghosts of those Airborne men will be forever in those woods, fields and houses of
Arnhem. Each year on September 17th they will be patrolling the places in the dark
with grimy, dirty faces, but grinning to each other, for it is theirs, all theirs – forever
Arnhem.

COUNTING MY BLESSINGS   185

THE BORDERERS' CHRONICLE.   5

A FAREWELL MESSAGE

5th (DUMFRIES AND GALLOWAY) BATTALION
6th (BORDER) BATTALION
7th (GALLOWAY) BATTALION

These three Battalions, having completed the tasks allotted to them in the War just ended, have now stood down. Each has passed into a state of "suspended animation," which means that although for the present they will have no posted strength their identity will be preserved, and should an opportunity occur at any time for them to be resuscitated, by the posting of personnel, they can be restored to an active role without formality or constitutional action.

Our 5th Battalion in the 52nd (Lowland) Division landed, for the second time, on the Continent in October, 1944, and immediately took part in the assault on Flushing. Then followed the battles of Dieteren, Waldfeucht, Broedersbosch, Ginderich, Hamminkeln and the operations beyond the River Rhine at Voltlage, Holtebuttel and Oyten, culminating in the capture of the great port of Bremen. It was at Flushing, Kievelburg, Waldfeucht, Broedersbosch, Voltage and Holtebuttel that the heaviest casualties were suffered. After their original assault on Walcheren Island, in the capture of Flushing, their Divisional Commander wrote of them (and of the 4th Battalion) :— "According to all the rules of War neither task should have been successful, but both Battalions went into it with such determination and sheer guts that nothing could have stopped them." This was not the only occasion on which they won high praise from him.

Our 6th Battalion in the 15th (Scottish) Division, landed in Normandy on D plus 8 day, in June, 1944, and had its first action in the battle of the "Scottish Corridor"—the breakthrough to the River Odon. The Battalion was then engaged in fierce fighting at St. Mauvieu and shortly afterwards gained distinction by holding off very fierce armoured counter-attacks in the region of L'Haut de Bosq. After taking a major part in the battle for the high ground at Point 113, overlooking Evrecy, they participated in the famous breakthrough by the 15th (Scottish) Division from Gaumont to the Bois d' Homme. On Minden Day; 1944, they attacked, as their forefathers in the Regiment had done in 1759, wearing roses in their headdress. After some dogged fighting at Estry, in Normandy, they took part in the northward race through Belgium. Assaulting the River Seine at Louviers they reached the Escaut Canal, north of Gheel, in September, 1944, and held a bridgehead against determined and persistent attacks by the enemy. Then northwards towards Eindhoven they took part in further fighting, culminating in the capture of Tilburg. Western Holland, near the River Maas, was the next scene of operations and then followed the capture of Blerick, in which the Battalion took a prominent part. In early 1945 came the assault from Nijmegen through the Siegfried Line into Germany. In their deep and speedy penetration of the Siegfried Defences, to capture the steep Matterborn feature and the key to Cleves the Battalion gained for itself the distinction of being one of the first of the Units of 21st Army Group to pass through the main Siegfried defences. Shortly afterwards they took a major part in the capture of Goch during which the rushing of the anti-tank ditch by night in armoured

troop carriers was of particular interest. A hard fought and highly successful action in the woods north of the River Niers between Goch and Weeze was the last action before the assault across the River Rhine in March 1945. This great obstacle was crossed near Xanten immediately in rear of two assault Battalions ; 6th Battalion then effected a deep penetration to the River Issel, capturing nearly 600 prisoners and being the first ground Unit to link up with the Airborne troops who had landed in advance. Finally came the assault across the River Elbe in April, 1945. The total casualties suffered were 1150.

Our 7th Battalion, in the First British Airborne Division, fought at Arnhem. Landing in gliders behind the enemy's lines on Sunday, 17th September, 1944, for nine consecutive days they fought magnificently against overwhelming odds. Their casualties were heavy, but their achievements were great; and that gallant action has added another glorious page to the history of our Regiment. In the early morning of Tuesday, 26th September, 4 Officers and 72 other ranks, all that remained of that splendid Battalion which had gone into action for the first time, crossed the swollen river and joined up with the British Force, south of the River, which had been battling its way northward to relieve them.

During those nine days many a gallant Borderer laid down his life. Fortunately, a large number of the wounded and missing have returned home since the conclusion of hostilities.

After Arnhem the 7th Battalion returned to England to re-form. They were subsequently flown to Norway in May, 1945 ; this time on a more peaceful mission.

Each Battalion in turn won fame and each was thanked by its Divisional Commander for the splendid way they had fought. All have well and truly accomplished the tasks which they were set and all have added glory to the history of our Regiment. We are proud of their achievements and we shall not forget those gallant men who will never return. Their deeds will be recorded in the History which we are now preparing of the War 1939-45.

Whatever the future may hold for our 5th, 6th and 7th Battalions we shall always remember the part they played in the winning of final victory. The Regiment takes leave of them, with sorrow at their parting but with pride in their achievements. We must ensure that this magnificent spirit which animated them and the friendships which grew amongst them, are perpetuated in the future. To all who fought with them we send a message of gratitude and we wish them Good Luck.

Our 1st, 2nd and 4th Battalions remain in the field, respectively in Palestine, in India and in Germany, and it is to be hoped that Borderers still serving will find themselves posted to one or other of these Battalions.

E. G. MILES, *Major-General*,
Colonel, The King's Own Scottish Borderers.

1st March, 1946.

The Borderers Chronicle, Volume 21, No 1, 30 March 1946
(Courtesy Robert Sigmond)

Appendix I

Tributes

A German tribute to the men of Arnhem:

They are certainly hardy fellows, the pick of the bunch, to whom the British Command entrusted the difficult operations at Arnhem. They are of all sorts and professions, age and origin – blacksmiths, bus conductors and students. There are men from London, Wales, Scotland and Canada.

When they are captured they smile, and if they are wounded they hide their pain. The paratroopers have already been driven from the bridge where they landed and held their first positions. But they fight on stubbornly.

By a war reporter over the German radio, on 27th September, 1944

Australian tribute:

If, in the years to come, any man says to you – 'I fought at Arnhem' – take off your hat to him and buy him a drink, for his is the stuff of which England's greatness is made.

By a newspaper reporter, Alan Wood,
who accompanied the 1st Allied Airborne Army

… ponder over the fierce fire that consumed the hearts and souls and minds of these men, an abstract flame of something to do with duty and love of country and self-preservation which made them fight like devils possessed.

'Piece of Cake', by Geoff Taylor

These were men of no ordinary calibre. They had been nine days in that little space, being mortared and shelled, machine-gunned and sniped from all round. When a tank or a self-propelled 88 gun broke through, two or three of them de-tached themselves and somehow or another had put it out of business.

For the last three days they had had no water, but very little small arms am-munition, and rations cut to one-sixth. Luckily, or unluckily, it rained, and they caught the water in their caps and drank that. These last items were never mentioned – they were airborne, weren't they? They were tough and knew it.

By a B.B.C. correspondent, Stanley Maxted, who landed with the Division

In the annals of the British Army there are many glorious deeds. In our Army we have always drawn great strength and inspiration from past traditions, and endeavoured to live up to the high standards of those who have gone before.

But there can be few episodes more glorious than the epic of Arnhem, and those that follow after will find it hard to live up to the high standards that you have set.

So long as we have in the armies of the British Empire, officers and men who will do as you have done, then we can indeed look forward with complete confidence to the future.

In years to come it will be a great thing for a man to be able to say: 'I fought at Arnhem.'

From a letter written to General Urquhart on the 28th September 1944
by Field-Marshall Montgomery

Appendix II

Operational Orders for Market-Garden

It may be of interest to show some of the 7th KOSB operational orders for Market-Garden:

Intention
7th KOSB will:-
(a) Protect DY Y until 4th Brigade Brigade are clear.
(b) Occupy reserve position in Brigade area and protect LZ L until Polish Parachute Brigade are clear.

Method-Phase I
7th KOSB will land on north end of LZ S at H Hour, less carriers, 5 ammunition jeeps and trailers and one Platoon C Company.
RV and check point 653826.

Phase II
4th Parachute Brigade is dropping on DZ Y at X Hour on D+1. 156th Battalion will land first and move into B Company area, 10th Battalion will land second and move into A Company area and 11th Battalion on landing will come in area of Battalion HQ. As soon as 4th Parachute Brigade have concentrated they will move and take up defensive positions in Arnhem.

Withdrawal
(a) A Company will co-ordinate their withdrawal with 4th Parachute Brigade and move to protect LZ L until 1st Polish Parachute Brigade Glider element has landed. A Company will withdraw to main Battalion position down the same axis as 1st Polish Parachute Brigade, when 1st Polish Parachute Brigade is clear of LZ.
(b) B and C Companies will co-ordinate their withdrawal with 4th Parachute Brigade under orders of the CO. There will be no withdrawal without orders from Battalion HQ.
(c) D Company, plus two sections mortars, one Platoon MMG and one Platoon Anti-Tank will remain in position until B and C Companies have passed through.
(d) B Company Group will move back to Bound 'Poor' and take up defensive positions with support weapons.
(e) C Company will pass through B Company Group and move straight back to Battalion positions in Arnhem.
(f) D Company will then move back through B Company and back to its position in Arnhem.
(g) B Company will move back when all troops have passed through and take up its position in Arnhem.
   Above bounds and Battalion main position in Arnhem will be recced during Phase I.

Further Reading

Over the years many books have been written either with the Battle of Arnhem as its central theme or having the fighting as a major part of the narrative. In my opinion one of the best general accounts (if not the best), would have to be Martin Middlebrook *Arnhem 1944: The Airborne Battle, 17-26 September,* London, Penguin Books Ltd, 1995. However in recent years there have been several excellent 'unit histories' produced and I would recommend any interested readers to look for the two written about the 7th KOSB:

Robert Sigmond *Off at Last: An Illustrated History of the 7th (Galloway) Battalion The King's Own Scottish Borderers 1939-194,* Renkum, The Netherlands, Sigmond Publishing, 1997

Robert Sigmond *Nine Days at Arnhem: Canadian Officers under the CANLOAN Scheme in the 7th (Galloway) Battalion The King's Own Scottish Borderers 1944-1945, 1st British Airborne Division,* Renkum, The Netherlands, Sigmond Publishing, 2004

Other Corps and Regimental books that may be of interest are as follows:

Roberts, J. *With Spanners Descending: Short History of the Royal Electrical and Mechanical Engineers with 1st Airborne Division, 1942-45,* Liverpool, The Bluecoat Press, 1996

Roekel, C van *The Torn Horizon: The Airborne Chaplains at Arnhem,* N.p. 2000. [This book mentions Reverend Morrison on numerous occasions]

Cherry, N. *Red Berets and Red Crosses: Story of the Medical Services in the 1st Airborne Division in World War Two,* Renkum, The Netherlands, Sigmond Publishing, 1999. [This book includes information on Captain Devlin and his replacement Captain Kaye]

Niall Cherry, 2004

The Airborne Museum 'Hartenstein' at Oosterbeek

The original Airborne Museum opened in 1949 when a number of private collections of artefacts relating to the Battle of Arnhem were brought together and exhibited in Doorwerth Castle in the village of Renkum a few miles away from Oosterbeek. In 1977 the Hotel Hartenstein closed and the building was re-opened in 1978 as the Airborne Museum Hartenstein. This building had in September 1944 been the Headquarters of the 1st Airborne Division and so was an entirely appropriate place for the unique 'Arnhem Museum' to be located. The Museum has remained in Oosterbeek ever since then and through its unique collection of artefacts, photographs and documents paints a penetrating picture of the story of the Battle of Arnhem in September 1944. Certain events of the Battle are brought to life by a number of dioramas using original equipment and clothing. Over the years numerous veterans and others have donated items and some of the prize exhibits include John Frost's hunting horn, Brigadier Hackett's beret and the Pegasus pennant taken by General Urquhart to Arnhem. Each year it attracts over 50,000 visitors. The Museum has a thriving and active Society of Friends which support the Museum in a number of activities. It produces a quarterly newsletter which contains news and articles about the Battle and each issue contains a 'Ministory' in which a specific aspect of the Battle is examined in detail. 2005 sees the 25th anniversary of the Friends. Further information on the Museum can be found on the internet at www.airbornemuseum.com and the Friends UK representative is N Cherry and he can be contacted at 3 Church Road Warton Lancs PR4 1BD. The Museum is open between April and November from 10-00 till 17-00 and outside these months 11-00 till 17-00. On Sundays and public holidays 12-00 till 17-00. A small admission charge is payable although veterans and members of the Society of Friends have free admission.

Related titles published by Helion & Company

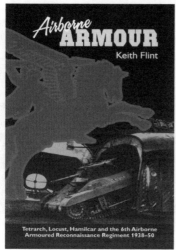

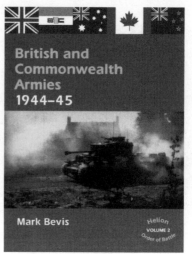

Airborne Armour. Tetrarch, Locust, Hamilcar and the 6th Airborne Armoured Reconnaissance Regiment 1938-50
Keith Flint
224pp   Hardback
ISBN 1 874622 37 X

British & Commonwealth Armies 1944-45
(Helion Order of Battle series volume 2)
Mark Bevis
96pp   Paperback
ISBN 1 874622 90 6

A selection of forthcoming titles

An Active Service: The Story of a Soldier's Life in the Grenadier Guards & SAS 1935-58
Richard Dorney   ISBN 1 874622 48 5

British & Commonwealth Armies, 1939-45 Supplement Volume 1
(Helion Order of Battle series volume 3)
Mark Bevis   ISBN 1 874622 18 3

British & Commonwealth Armies, 1939-45 Supplement Volume 2
(Heliobn Order of Battle series volume 4)
Mark Bevis   ISBN 1 874622 38 8

Penalty Strike: The Memoirs of a Red Army Penal Company Commander 1943-45
Alexander V. Pyl'cyn   ISBN 1 874622 63 9

Red Star Airacobra. Memoirs of a Soviet Fighter Ace 1941-45
Evgeniy Mariinskiy ISBN 1 874622 78 7

HELION & COMPANY LIMITED
26 Willow Road, Solihull, West Midlands, B91 1UE, England
Tel 0121 705 3393   Fax 0121 711 4075
Website: http://www.helion.co.uk